CALLED TO SUCCEED

MY FIRST WORDS TO YOU

I have written this book for you. It has been a labor of love. It contains my stories, teachings, testimony, miracles, heartbreak and success. I am not sharing with you what I have heard or read somewhere. I'm sharing what I have lived.

My prayer is that you learn from my experiences, apply these biblically based principles to your life and fully live the life that God has intended for you.

My wife and I are here for you. If you need some help, contact us. My call in life is to help you fulfill your call and purpose on this earth. There is more to life than "just getting by."

God is no respecter of persons. He does not love me more than He loves you. He does not have a better plan for me than He has for you.

This is your time! This is your season! You do not have this book by chance. This is in the divine plan of God. Receive all that God has intended for you!

"Always be content but never be complacent!"
-Calvin Washington

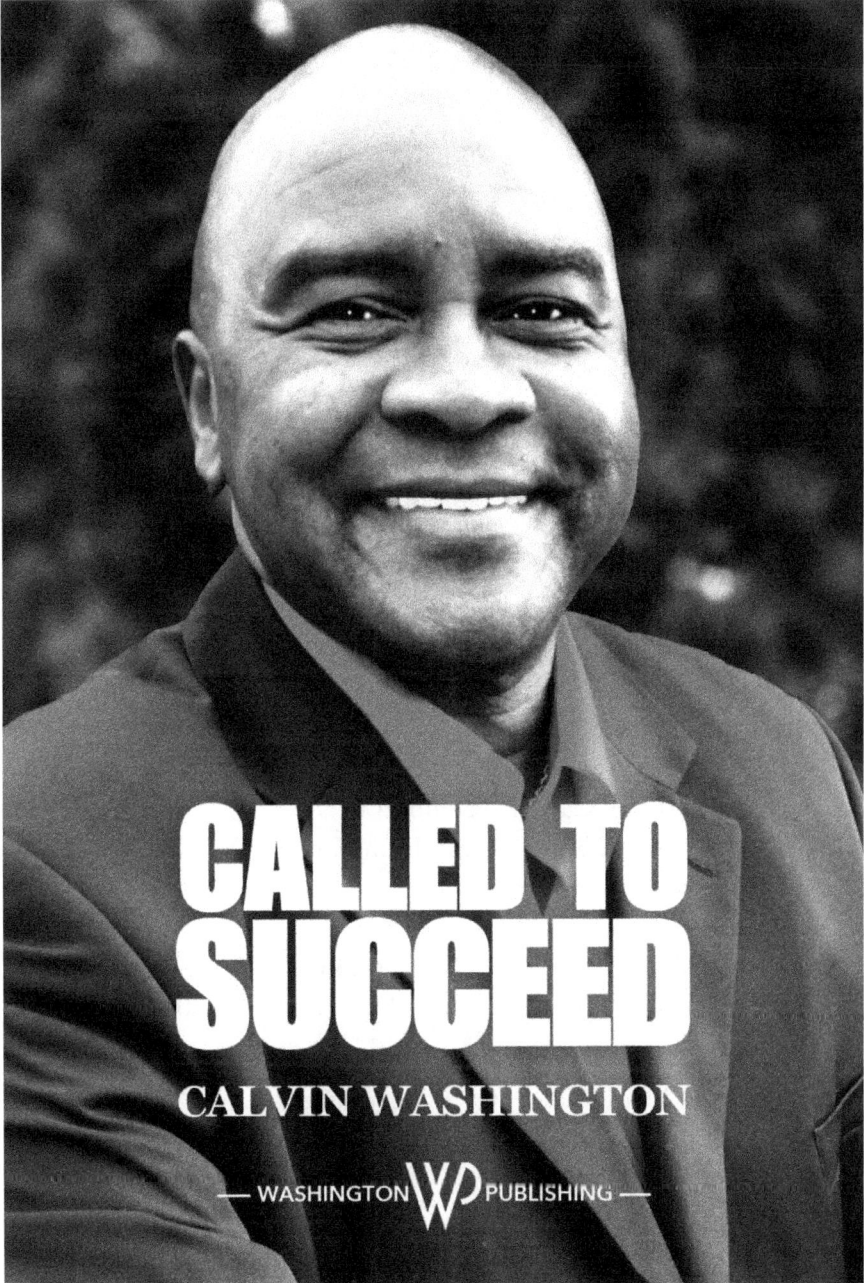

CALLED TO SUCCEED

CALVIN WASHINGTON

— WASHINGTON W PUBLISHING —

The author may have emphasized some words in italicized type or bold within the Scripture quotations. These words are not emphasized in the original Bible versions.

Take note that the name satan and related names are not capitalized as we do not recognize him as neither supreme nor revered to the point of violating grammatical rules. Conversely, any reference to God, Jesus and/or the Holy Spirit (He, Him, You, etc.) will always be capitalized, to the point of violating grammatical rules because they refer to Supreme Beings.

CALLED TO SUCCEED   ISBN 978-0-9774258-0-8

Copyright © 2013 by Calvin Washington
11877 Douglas Road, Suite 102213, Johns Creek, GA 30005
www.calvinwashington.com

Published by Washington^{wp} Publishing, LLC.
11877 Douglas Road, Suite 102213, Johns Creek, GA 30005

Creative Direction, Cover Design and Photography:
Devon Chénee Media, LLC. www.devonchenee.com

DEDICATION

I dedicate this book to my loving wife and partner for life,
Nicole. Thank you for all your love and prayers that have
helped me in our journey together. You are my true love, best
friend and my prayer warrior.
I also dedicate this book to my loving children:
Cimmerian, Nikolai, Nikolette and
my loving Goddaughter, Devon.
Everyday I breathe; I am purposing to leave
a legacy you all will be proud of.

I greatly love each of you!

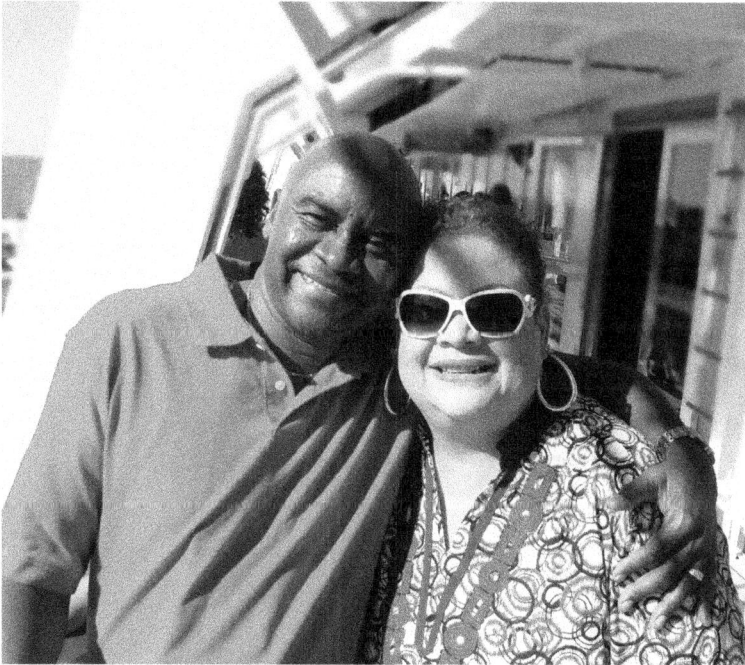

STOP! IMPORTANT! READ!

If Jesus Christ is *not* the Lord of your life and if you are not *absolutely* sure of where you will spend eternity (heaven or hell), please read this simple prayer out loud, sincerely from your heart:

Father God, I believe Jesus is Your Son. I believe He died for me and rose again from the dead. I believe Jesus is alive right now, seated beside You in heaven. I confess that I am a sinner. I repent for all my sins and ask You to forgive me. I ask You Jesus, to come into my heart now, as I yield my life to You. Thank You Lord Jesus, for loving me and saving me.

In the name of Jesus, I pray. Amen!

"If you declare that Jesus is Lord and believe that God brought him back to life, you will be saved."
Romans 10:9 (GW)

Many spend their lifetime searching for success,

you have just answered its first call.

CONGRATULATIONS!

Welcome to the kingdom of God.

CONTENTS

Forward   9

Preface   13

Freedom Assured   16

1   What Is Success?   17

2   Are You Called?   21

3   Learning To Succeed   25

4   Attitude For Success   35

5   Success Through Your Words   47

6   Success Through Godliness   61

7   Success Through Spiritual Weapons   69

8   Success Through Giving   85

9   Success Through Prayer   98

10   How To Mature In The Call   117

11   Success Blockers   131

12   God's Will Regarding Money   143

13   Be Encouraged!   158

14   Take Action   167

15   Everybody's Got A Cotton Field   181

16   My Final Words   205

17   Calvin Washington   209

"Every great dream begins
with a dreamer. Always remember,
you have within you the strength,
the patience and the passion
to reach for the stars to
change the world."

-Harriet Tubman

FORWARD

I have known Apostle Calvin Washington for over ten years and I have experienced the miracles and power of God flow through his life first hand. My life has tremendously changed under his teachings of godly success and I have benefited in so many ways. I could write a book about all the miracles, enlightenment, spiritual lessons and enormous blessings I have received through this great ministry.

Through his teachings, prayer and mentorship offered over the years, Apostle Washington opened my eyes to a life of faith, power, victory, success and triumphant living through God's Word. Since being exposed to these teachings, I have gone from poverty to prosperity and from sickness to divine health.

Although, my life has changed under his ministry in many different ways, I have one miracle that stands out the most. Each time I reflect on this event, I tear up and become overwhelmed with praise at the wondrous works of God through Apostle Washington.

On the birthdate of my second son, Kendall, I witnessed a wonderful and remarkable miracle. My wife was admitted to the hospital early due to several complications. After many hours of waiting, the doctor determined the baby was not going to be born that day.

Through a routine examination and mishap by one of the nurses, my wife went into active labor and their decision to send my wife home immediately changed. During the process of labor, my unborn son went into great medical distress. In all my years of being at a hospital, I have *never, ever* seen doctors or nurses so panicked. I knew I had to call Apostle Washington, so I called him right away to advise him of what was going on.

He quickly said, "Let's pray and put your wife on speaker phone." I did so immediately. *I will never forget this as long as I live.* He specifically said, "George, you *must* place your hand on your wife's abdomen (on the baby) before we pray." When I had my hands in place, he began to pray; however this prayer was different from his usual methods of praying. He began to shout, "Jesus, Jesus, Jesus, Jesus!"

Calling on Jesus was the entirety of the prayer, for about ten minutes! My son's heart rate had been dropping fast and my wife was in excruciating pain. Apostle kept saying repeatedly, "Jesus, Jesus, Jesus!" It began to sound like a shouting cry. Suddenly, my son's heart rate began to increase and finally, his heartbeat became normal!

After the prayer, my wife gave birth to my son but he still was not totally in the clear. He was not breathing normally and the nurse did all she could to try to revive him to no avail. All I could remember was the prayer Apostle Washington prayed.

Repeatedly, he called on Jesus the healer, so I did too. After calling on that name...Jesus, Jesus, Jesus...over and over, the change in my newborn son was like night and day. Kendall began to breathe normally, cry and even scream - the best sounds I had ever heard!

This testimonial just shows us what God Almighty can do through a yielded and committed vessel like Apostle Washington. He has taught me that success is not just about money but also about success in marriage, health, relationships, childbirth and all areas of life!

This book will be a life changer for you as you read it. The revelations contained herein are proven to be true. I know this because they have been proven in my life!

My wife and I give glory, honor and praise to God for His love, grace and mercy. Jesus is the resurrection and the life and we thank Him for placing a true Apostle of God in our lives. Thanks forever, Apostle Washington!

Pastor George H. Johnson, Jr.
The Way of Success Ministries
McDonough, GA

"Almost everybody has a story but it's important to find someone who has a story that will not only uplift your spirit but change your soul and ultimately your life.
Calvin Washington
has that story."

-Nicole Y. Washington

PREFACE

Why Do People Call Me Apostle?

Many people have asked me why I am referred to as Apostle instead of Pastor now. I've heard many times, "Apostles don't exist anymore. They were only in the Bible" and "Do you think you're like Apostle Paul?"

Nobody, Paul included, can be an Apostle in the way the original twelve were. According to Revelation 21:14, there are only 12 original Apostles and the Lamb, Jesus.

I have taught the Bible and pastored for many years and many Pastors consider me to be their Pastor; however God has called me now, as an Apostle.

1 Corinthians 12:28 (NLT)
*"Here is a list of some of the members that God has placed in the body of Christ: first are **apostles**, second are prophets, third are teachers, then those who do miracles, those who have the gift of healing, those who can help others, those who can get others to work together, those who speak in unknown languages."*

The Greek word APOSTOLOS translated Apostle, means one sent forth**, a sent one.** When I left Montgomery, Alabama, I was *"sent"* and instructed to establish additional ministries and churches for which I had oversight responsibility.

The Bible speaks of the signs of an Apostle:

2 Corinthians 12:12 (NIV)
*"The things that mark an Apostle-**signs, wonders and miracles-**
were done among you with great perseverance.*

The indicators of an Apostle are signs, wonders and miracles. God has blessed my ministry to have these manifest in profound measure, many of which you will read about in this book. My experience with God is very deep and real, it is NOT just some title handed down by a tradition or a "religious" promotion. Paul had to defend his position of Apostle:

1 Corinthians 9:1 (KJV)
*"**Am I not an apostle?** Am I not free? Have I not seen Jesus Christ our Lord? Are not ye my work in the Lord?"*

Did Paul literally, *physically* see Jesus as the original twelve did? NO! He saw Jesus in the *spirit* realm. He had a deep *spiritual experience* with the Lord.

Additionally, there are many people the Bible refers to as "Apostle" that were *not* part of the original twelve that *literally* walked with Jesus. Here are some others:

Acts 14:14 - **Barnabas** and **Paul**
Galatians 1:19 - **James** (brother of Jesus)
Romans 16:7 - **Andronicus** and **Junia** (a woman)
Thessalonians 1:1; 2:6 - **Silvanus** and **Timotheus**
1 Corinthians 4:4-9 - **Apollos**

2 Corinthians 8:23 - **Two unidentified people** (the word translated "messenger" is the same Greek word translated "Apostle" in other places).

So what should we look for in people who are called as an Apostle *today*? According to the Word, there are four specific things:

Outstanding spiritual gifts, signs, wonders and mighty deeds (2 Corinthians 12:12).

Deep personal experience demonstrated by evidence of the fruit of the Spirit (1 Corinthians 9).

Power and ability to establish churches (1 Corinthians 3:6-10).

Ability to provide spiritual leadership to places sent (Acts 13:2, 4).

That is the person to whom God bestows the title Apostle. Remember, God rewards faithfulness, He doesn't reward offices.

Holding an office does not mean you receive any more reward; it only means you have greater responsibility!

FREEDOM ASSURED

"Events that injure come our way.
We bring them to pass in what we say.
We set in motion events that ensnare.
We call them burdens and say they're unfair.
The tongue in motion is a raging fire.
It separates man from his greatest desire.
Hard can be the webs we weave,
So confounded it's hard to believe.
Just as gravity holds us down,
That which circles comes back around.
As the earth revolves and waters flow,
From good and bad we reap what we sow.
All produce after their kind,
Through words, through deeds
And through the mind.
As strong as the tides of the glistening ocean,
Are the good and the bad we set in motion.
Whatever the challenge or problem may be,
The Lord and His Word will set you free!"

-Calvin Washington

1

WHAT IS SUCCESS?

Nobody's answer to this question is going to be the same all the time. Most of us are in a constant state of ebb and flow, defining or redefining our answer based on the circumstances of the day, month or year.

If you were to ask 1000 random people across the world how they define success (according to the average survey), answers will generally be related to getting more money, reaching goals and dreams, having clout, favor, status or power. You'll hear, folks say that being wealthy means being financially secure, being surrounded by people who take orders and serve. You'll hear, "Rich people enjoy the best of everything life has to offer!"

HOW DOES THE BIBLE DEFINE GOOD SUCCESS?

Joshua 1:8 (KJV)
*"This book of the law shall not depart out of thy mouth; that thou shalt **meditate** therein day and night, that thou mayest observe to do according to all that is written therein: for then thou shalt make thy way **prosperous** and then thou shalt have **good success.**"*

Do you remember the story of David and Solomon? Well, when King David was near death, he told his son Solomon,

1 Kings 2:3 (CEV)
*"Do what the LORD your God commands and follow his teachings. Obey everything written in the Law of Moses. Then you will be a **success, no matter what you do or where you go.***"

Remember the importance of these words. They are some of the last words David spoke to Solomon. They are weighty and very important. David didn't tell his son anything about war and conquering land or to build up his kingdom with great armies or to gather wealth from other lands or to defeat his enemies in battle. That's what most great rulers would say in their dying breath. But not David!

David, in essence, said *follow God* and *obey Him*, then *success will follow you*! The Bible tells us that when Solomon did become King, he did not ask God for wealth or power or more kingdoms. He obeyed his father's last words. Solomon asked God for wisdom and discernment to lead God's people. Obviously, God was pleased by Solomon's request, because He honored it. God caused Solomon to have a very wise and understanding heart. Along with having the greatest wisdom of all humanity, God also gave Solomon riches and honor among men:

1 Kings 3:9-14 (NLT)
"Give me an understanding mind so that I can govern your people well and know the difference between right and wrong. For who by himself is able to govern this great nation of yours?" [10] *The Lord*

*was pleased with Solomon's reply and was glad that he had **asked for wisdom**. [11] So God replied, "Because you have asked for wisdom in governing my people and have not asked for a long life or riches for yourself or the death of your enemies. [12] I will give you what you asked for! I will give you a wise and understanding mind such as no one else has ever had or ever will have! [13] And I will also **give you what you did not ask for riches and honor**! No other king in all the world will be compared to you for the rest of your life! [14] And if you follow me and obey my commands as your father, David, did, I will give you a long life."*

Solomon was steadfast in following his father's instructions (mostly), before faltering and stumbling. As Solomon aged, he reflected on his father's words in his writings in Proverbs:

Proverbs 3:1-4 (ESV)

*"My son, do not forget my teaching but let your heart keep my commandments, for length of days and years of life and peace they will add to you. Let not steadfast love and faithfulness forsake you; bind them around your neck; write them on the tablet of your heart. So **you will find favor and good success** in the sight of God and man."*

In Joshua 1:8, Joshua wrote that God said, "This Book of the Law shall not depart from your mouth but you shall meditate in it day and night, that you may observe to do according to all that is written in it. For then *you will make your way prosperous and have good success.*

"Believe you can and you're halfway there."
–Theodore Roosevelt

SUCCESS IS A BIBLE WORD

The original Hebrew word translated success in this verse is **SAKAL** (saw-kal'). In Strong's Concordance #7913, it is defined as: to be prudent, be circumspect, wisely understand, to prosper, to look at or upon, have insight, to give attention to, consider, ponder, have comprehension, to cause to consider, teach the teachers, the wise, act wisely, to prosper, have success, to cause to prosper.

Joshua 1:8 (AMP)
*"This Book of the Law shall not depart out of your mouth but you shall meditate on it day and night, that you may observe and do according to all that is written in it. For then you shall make your way prosperous and then you shall deal wisely and have **good success**."*

In the Amplified Bible, the last part of Joshua 1:8 reads, "deal wisely and have *good success*." Prudent means wise. Wise means knowing what to do. That's success!

Psalm 1:1-3 (NIV)
*"Blessed is the one who does not walk in step with the wicked or stand in the way that sinners take or sit in the company of mockers but whose delight is in the law of the LORD and who meditates on his law day and night. That person is like a tree planted by streams of water, which yields its fruit in season and whose leaf does not wither – **whatever they do prospers**."*

"Success comes in cans, not in cannots."
– Anonymous

2

ARE YOU CALLED?

"The test of a preacher is that his congregation goes away saying, not what a lovely sermon but, I will do something!"
- St. Francis de Sales

When I was a little boy growing up and working in the cotton fields of central Texas, the world looked very small to me. I had no idea there were about 2.3 billion people in the world! Of course, those days were before the internet. Now, I can search the internet!

I had a vague idea of what being called by God was in those days. I knew my mother was called. She was a very committed, godly woman and a member of the Church of God in Christ, affectionately referred to as C.O.G.I.C. I knew her Pastor was called to the ministry. Other than that, I didn't give much thought to it - especially none to my *ever* being called by God.

There are now over 7 billion people on earth. Of that number, 2.2 billion people believe - in some way or another - in the name of Jesus Christ. This group of people represents over 2,000 different forms of professed Christianity. Now, I have no problem telling you that many of them, I would run away from like the plague! Remember, the enemy has proliferated many forms of false religion all over the earth. He counterfeits the truth in endless ways and God's calling process is no exception. He is a master deceiver and the evidence of his work is everywhere. Approximately another 2.5 billion have heard of Jesus but have not claimed to follow Him. The other third either has not heard of Him at all or just outright reject Him. So what can we make of this?

WHO CHOOSES?

Jesus said it in John 15:16 (GW), "You didn't choose me but I chose you." And guess what? Any employer could say that to his employee! When there is a position available, companies put out an ad or announcement for the job. Let's say you applied for the job. You had to agree to work for the company but they couldn't force themselves on you. In the final analysis, the employer could say, "You didn't choose me, I chose you." In other words, "You can't *make* me hire you."

On the other hand, the employer couldn't make you work for his company either. That would be slave labor. So, Jesus draws everybody, He desires everybody, He *is not* willing that anybody should perish and He would have all men come to the knowledge of the truth. He will not force you or drag you into His kingdom. He will let us choose.

In other words, Jesus calls to everybody because He gave His life for *everybody*! Jesus says in the Bible, "Come to Me, all you who labor and are heavy laden and I will give you rest" (Matthew 11:28). There are about 2.2 billion people today who do *not* want to do that! Considering the numbers, obviously *everybody is not* going to be a Believer. God is simply not going to force people to become Christians. I submit to you, He *is* calling them to be.

THOSE WHO HAVE BEEN CALLED

1. Thessalonians: "The one who calls you is faithful."
   1 Thessalonians 5:24 (GW)
2. Paul wrote: "I'm surprised that you're so quickly deserting Christ, who called you in his kindness, to follow a different kind of good news." Galatians 1:6 (GW) and later, "The arguments of the person who is influencing you do not come from the one who is calling you." Galatians 5:8 (GW)
3. To the Corinthians the Bible says, "Brothers and sisters, consider what you were when God called you to be Christians." 1 Corinthians 1:26 (GW)

When we look at all these scriptures together, it explains that God is calling a *few* people—a very few—out of the world for His Supreme Purpose. Those who respond, to His calling, are "chosen", then prayerfully on to repentance, conversion and baptism in the Holy Spirit. As we review the Bible, we can see that there are several types of callings:

1. **Called to Salvation** - That's the one we were just referencing. God reaches out to all people to reestablish the relationship that was destroyed by sin and the fall of man. Of course, God would be ecstatic if everybody accepted Jesus as

Lord and Savior; but He gave us a free will to choose and some folks choose to *not* accept.

2. **Called to Godliness** - Once we have been reconciled to God through salvation, He then calls us to godliness. This means, He sets us apart for His purposes. Nobody is perfect. Truly, there is one and that is Jesus. God already knows we won't live perfect lives but we are supposed to aim in that direction as best we can. Meaning, we should choose to live toward righteousness and obedience to the Word.

3. **Called to Serve** - God has chosen to carry out His work in the world through people like us. Although there are ministry gifts (Apostles, Prophets, Evangelists, Pastors and Teachers), every person who claims Jesus as Lord and Savior, is in a sense, a minister of the gospel of Jesus Christ.

4. **Called to Succeed** - John 10:10, "The thief cometh not but for to steal and to kill and to destroy: I am come that they might have life and that they might have it more abundantly."

I submit to you that God has a remnant of His people that will operate in all that He has *called* them to. They will have a life of GOOD success, a life full of happiness, peace, joy, love and a life of abundance. Jesus came so *"they"* would have life and have it more abundantly. Who does "they" refer to? It refers to us! We are the "they"! **You and I are called to succeed because of Jesus!** All we have to do is appropriate His great work, on the cross of Calvary, to our lives today.

3

LEARNING TO SUCCEED

"We should not judge people by their peak of excellence; but by the distance they have traveled from the point where they started."
-Henry Ward Beecher

Many years ago, I took a look at all the struggles and hardships that I was facing and I began to wonder what in the world was happening to me. It made me begin to wonder why God allowed so much injustice, sickness, evil and trouble to take place in this world. Over the years, I received a good education and had become a fairly successful attorney.

During that period of my life, I lived in the Washington, D.C. area. I found that even though education and the practice of law were great and rewarding, there were still many problems that education and law just could not solve. One day I was so frustrated with my life, I told a friend of mine that I was going to seek and search until I found some answers and solutions to many of life's troubling and perplexing problems. She told me it was foolish of me to think I could get any clear-cut answers to questions that have frustrated millions of people for years. She had no idea what she had just set in motion. I have long taken the position that when people tell me I can't achieve or reach a certain goal; it's like saying sick'em to a bulldog! Unbeknownst to her, she had just given me more incentive to succeed. So, I set out to prove her wrong.

LIGHT COMES TO DARKNESS

For many years I searched for answers, wondering whether there was more to life than getting up, facing the world, going to work, paying the bills and doing the same things year after year. I sought answers in eastern mysticism, various self-help gurus and seminars. I can't count the many books I have bought that were supposed to provide answers to the challenges and questions of life. Nothing that I did brought me true joy or fulfillment.

After experiencing so many problems–including sickness and other hardships–I called up another friend who had been telling me for many weeks that I needed to come to Jesus. That advice went in one ear and out the other. I thought I could solve all of my problems, on my own, without getting involved in religion.

I had shunned religion all my life because I felt that it didn't really work.   All the people that talked to me about Jesus appeared worse off in life than me! My mother was a righteous woman but many times I saw her victimized by so many injustices and hardships that I thought I could do better *without* religion. I had gone to church on many occasions but I felt that many churchgoers were hypocritical, phony or out of step with the times. Being so frustrated with all the hardships I was facing, I called my friend who had been trying to get me to turn my life over to the Lord. I told my friend I was going through many problems and *nobody* seemed to have any answers. Finally, I threw up my hands and decided I'd tried everything else, *why not* try this, "Jesus thing."

The problems I wanted to talk about were truly overwhelming. She realized what I was going through and had gotten involved in was too much for her to handle. So, she referred me to another minister who lived in another state, many miles away.

TIME TO GIVE UP

I called the number she gave me. The minister told me the only way I was going to get out of my mess and frustrations was to accept Jesus as my Lord and Savior. At that point I thought, "Here we go again with this religion business." He said, "Do you want to accept Jesus?" I paused a long time, feeling hopeless and finally said, "Yes, sir."

He prayed with me and I accepted Jesus as my Lord and Savior. The scripture says, "Because if you confess with your mouth that Jesus is Lord and believe in your heart that God raised him from the dead, you will be saved" (Romans 10:9 ESV). I had confessed Jesus as my Lord and Savior and I became saved!

OLD HABITS DIE HARD

After accepting Jesus, I thought I could continue life as usual by trying to solve my own problems and not really reading or following biblical principles. After all, I had seen many churchgoers living the same way I had been living, *except* they went to church more often. I stumbled and fumbled around trying to understand what was necessary to be a committed Believer in the Lord Jesus Christ.

Several people kept telling me I needed to be truly committed to God. One person told me I needed to be "grounded and rooted in the Lord." Believers told me I needed to be a doer of God's Word and not just a hearer *only*. They said I was a Believer but I was still too "carnal" meaning that, in many ways, I acted just like people who did not believe in Jesus.

The only committed role models that I had seen were my mother and many of the people in her church but I felt that all that praying, shouting and dancing was old fashioned. So, I continued to stumble and fumble, looking for answers; but this didn't last long.

GOD APPROACHED THE YEAR BEFORE

The Believers who kept telling me to become more committed to God reminded me of a group of people I met in Phoenix, Arizona a year or so before I came to Jesus. I had gone there to argue a legal case and while there, I met a number of people who were so radically dedicated to God, I found it hard to believe. I *knew* they had to be putting on a show for me, at least that's what I *thought*.

One of the men told me he and his wife had once had a terrible marriage but when he came to God, his marriage changed totally. His wife said she hated him before he accepted Jesus. He said he could not read or write but that God had done a strange work in his life by giving him the ability to read and understand only *one* book, the Holy Bible. I thought, what kind of Christianity is this? I had never seen anything like this before in my life.

The people invited me to their church. They showed me a great deal of love and quickly accepted me, even though they had never seen me before. It was graduation time and many of the graduates said they were going to attend Bible colleges and seminaries. This amazed me. I thought, "How could so many people be interested in studying religion?"

As I sat there, in church that Sunday, tears began to flow down my face during the sermon. I couldn't understand what was taking place. The people in Phoenix encouraged me to commit to the Lord the same way the people in Washington, D.C. would do a year later. One of the guys I met played professional football. That year, his team was the best team in professional football. I can't tell you how surprised I was. In my ignorance, I thought professional football players were too macho or too arrogant to be committed to God. Even though these people had only known me a few days, they took me to a going away dinner. The Pastor told me to call him. He said he would give me the name of a church in the D.C. area similar to his but I failed to follow up.

SAVED BUT STILL WEAK

As I explained before, the Believers in the Washington, D.C. area told me, after coming to God, I was supposed to live according to the Word of God. While I changed my lifestyle *some*, I still had not totally "sold out" to Jesus. All the while, I kept asking many questions because I didn't really know what was expected of me. During that time, I was never able to totally figure out exactly how to change my lifestyle. I wanted to; I just didn't know *how*.

I was still walking in carnality. What does this mean? It means that if God had given me a grade on my relationship with Him, it would have probably been a grade of a D or a very low C. I heard one person describe this type of behavior as having "one foot in the 'world' and the other foot in the Kingdom of God." But, I kept asking questions about how I was supposed to live.

One woman told me that God told her to leave me alone and that He (God) was going to teach me a lesson. At that point, I got quite nervous. I thought, "Oh, my goodness, what kind of lesson is God going to teach me?" I wondered if I was going to have a car wreck, have trouble on my job or fall and break my leg or something.

CARNALITY COMES TO A HALT

Late one night, when I was out on a date, I received what I can only describe as a vision. In the middle of the air, a Bible appeared and it seemed as if a hand were holding it up. It was just like a situation where you might say to someone, "Hey, pass me that Bible" and the other person laid the Bible in the palm of his hand and passed it to you.

The floating Bible, in the vision, had no hand holding it up and also had a burning candle on top of it. The floating Bible and candle gradually disappeared. All of a sudden, the number 121 flashed before my face and gradually faded away. I didn't know much about God or His mysteries but I knew to quickly get a Bible! Apparently, by divine inspiration, I was urged or moved to turn (in the King James version of the Bible) to Psalm 121 and read that scripture.

Psalm 121 (KJV)

"I will lift up my eyes to the hills—From whence comes my help? My help comes from the Lord, Who made heaven and earth. He will not allow your foot to be moved; He who keeps you will not slumber. Behold, He who keeps Israel Shall neither slumber nor sleep. The Lord is your keeper; The Lord is your shade at your right hand. The sun shall not strike you by day, Nor the moon by night.

The Lord shall preserve you from all evil; He shall preserve your soul. The Lord shall preserve your going out and your coming in from this time forth and even forevermore."

Amazingly, I had never read this scripture before. I was especially touched by the words, "I will lift up mine eyes unto the hills, from whence cometh my help" and "my help cometh from the Lord which made heaven and earth." I was also moved by the words, "The Lord is thy keeper" and "the Lord shall preserve thy going out and thy coming in from this time forth and even for evermore."

God was showing me that, according to the Bible, Psalm 119:130 (KJV), the "entrance" of God's "words giveth light" and "it giveth understanding to the simple." God was showing me, through the vision that I was supposed to follow His Word and He would help and enlighten me. After seeing the floating Bible and the burning candle and after reading Psalm 121, I left my date quickly, promptly, speedily, post haste and expeditiously! This means, I split that scene! I made a "beeline" toward my home and I turned my back on carnality, stumbling and fumbling!

GOD GIVES ME FREEDOM

After God showed me the vision of the Bible and the burning candle, I knew that I should become more dedicated to God and His Word. I wanted more of God and less of me, so I started reading Christian books, studying God's Word, fasting and listening to the teaching tapes of different ministers.

Once I started increasing my focus on God, I began to hear a loud ringing noise in my ears. The ringing was so loud and distracting, it was hard for me to study, concentrate or perform the duties on my job. I had to meet deadlines, do legal research and write legal briefs — so my workload was quite heavy. Additionally, I had to go to trial in federal court and make arguments regarding the legal briefs I'd written. My job was *very* stressful and *very* demanding to say the least!

WORKING WITH CLARENCE THOMAS

What made it even more stressful was the fact that I sometimes had to sit-in on executive level management meetings. In these meetings, officials appointed by the President of the United States, along with other executive managers, discussed important governmental business.

In those days, the highest ranked executive manager, on my job, was Clarence Thomas who had been appointed by the President to be the Chair (head of the agency). President George H. Bush later appointed Clarence Thomas to be a Supreme Court Justice of the United States. Clarence Thomas presided over the meetings and I had to monitor the meetings to make sure the discussions were legally proper.

The stress was exceptionally high. For all these reasons, I had to be able to speak well, focus, concentrate, stay alert and think clearly. The more I listened to the tapes by ministers, the louder the ringing in my ears became. That sound in my ears made it very hard for me to focus and concentrate. Day and night, I would be bothered by this loud, annoying and distracting ringing in my ears.

Then, I told a woman who was a very strong and dedicated follower of Jesus to pray for me. She prayed forcefully and fervently and the loud ringing in my ears just disappeared. This victory gave me an even stronger desire to serve and get closer to God.

"Success is speaking words of praise,
in cheering other people's ways;
in doing just the best you can
with every task and every plan.
It's silence when your speech would hurt.
Politeness when your neighbor's curt.
It's deafness when the scandals flow
and sympathy when others woe.
It's loyalty when duty calls.
It's courage when disaster falls.
It's patience when the nights are long.
It's found in laughter and in song,
in happiness and in despair.
In all of life and nothing less
we find the thing we call success."
–Unknown

4

ATTITUDE FOR SUCCESS

**"When everything seems to be going against you,
remember that the airplane takes off
against the wind, not with it."
–Henry Ford**

The dictionary defines attitude as the psychological response to people, society, objects, events, occurrences and circumstances to life itself. So what does that have to do with being called to succeed? Depending on whether your attitude is positive or negative – and what choices you make – attitude may be one of the *most important* factors in your life from this point on.

We all make choices. We can choose to entertain thoughts of self-encouragement and self-motivation or we can choose those of self-defeat and self-pity. It's a power God has given *all of us*. More often than not, we meet with hard times, hurt feelings, heartache, as well as, physical and emotional pain. The key is to realize it's not *what happens* to you that matters; it's how you choose to *respond*!

**"It is our attitude at the beginning of a difficult undertaking which,
more than anything else, will determine its successful outcome."
-William James**

WHAT IS A POSITIVE ATTITUDE?

Attitude is your general disposition, your "starting point" for viewing life and the people and events in it. From your viewpoint, attitude is the way *you* look at things and it all starts inside your head. For others, your attitude is the overall mood they interpret from what *they see you say and do.*

People usually respond well to a positive attitude and an optimistic person. Someone who always seems to anticipate good news and transmits a positive attitude can be a joy to be around. People, who expect the worst, project a negative attitude that speaks "louder than anything they can possibly say." It's a natural response for others to shy away from people who might make them feel negative.

NEGATIVE ATTITUDE

Think of attitude as the way you look at things, the way *your thoughts* focus on the world around you. When using the camera or camcorder, you can focus on whatever you want. You can focus or set your mind in the same way – to see either opportunity or trouble.

A difficult problem is either something for you to complain about or is an opportunity for you to show what you can do knowing God's got your back! A conversation with a friend can be a chance to explore new information or can become a gripe session. Your attitude is never static; it's always in a state of flux. You are always affected by what's going on around you. Events, circumstances and messages – both positive and negative – can affect your attitude. Emphasizing the positive is like using a magnifying glass. Place the glass over good news and feel better; or over bad news and make yourself and others feel miserable. What each person chooses to magnify can easily become a habit in that person's life. It only takes 30 days to form a habit!

~~~~~~~~~~~~~~~~~~~~

By adjusting your thoughts on a situation, to highlight God's Word and the positive, you'll often find that you're in a better position to deal with whatever it is, even if it's difficult or troublesome.

~~~~~~~~~~~

No one can be positive all the time but a positive attitude sure does make problem solving easier! The more *good* you expect from a situation, the more success you will achieve. Everyday, your attitude will *significantly* affect what you can see, what you can do and how you feel.

"An unexamined life is not worth living."
–Socrates

ATTITUDE MAKES A DIFFERENCE

Being with people who have a good attitude is like riding with the wind at your back. Being with people who have a negative attitude (worry warts) is like a Friday afternoon commute in downtown Atlanta, – it takes more energy and more time and there's always a greater chance that something bad will happen! People with a good attitude always seem to be looking up and looking forward.

People with this kind of attitude, will usually find that more opportunities will show up in their lives. They spot problems in time to take action and avoid major consequences. They will look out for you as a friend. They enjoy life. Don't forget, the attitude you bring with you every day will significantly affect what you can see, what you can do and how you feel!

POSITIVE ATTITUDE AND YOUR PERSONALITY

Have you ever heard people talk about a person they met who was very attractive, yet later they report how ugly the person really was because the person had a bad personality? *Your* personality exists in the *minds of others* and it is defined by each of them according to the way they view you. The way other people interpret your personality is a key factor in how they relate to you.

Their interpretation is not based on what *you* think you are, it's based on what *they* think you are. The impact of attitude is so great; it can overshadow a person's looks and his or her intelligence. If a positive attitude can be powerful enough to *enhance what* you think about someone, a negative attitude can do the same in reverse!

SOLVE DISPUTES QUICKLY

To be the most effective and most successful person you can be, you have got to solve personal conflicts quickly. If you have a conflict with someone, you may feel better if *you* take the initiative to deal with it; even if you feel the other person is more responsible for the situation than you are. If you allow a small problem to grow, it could eventually cause you to lose your positive attitude and open a spiritual door to your becoming bitter and resentful. If possible, try not to carry conflicts from one day to the next. The Bible says in Ephesians 4:26, *"Be angry without sinning. Don't go to bed angry" (GW).*

The tension that accompanies an unresolved conflict can eat away at your positive attitude. The longer it eats away; the more you stand to lose.

~~~~~~~~~~~~~~~~~~~
**When people behave unreasonably or unfairly,
take the high road; don't drop to their level!**
~~~~~~~~~~~

Obviously, there are some issues and values where you have to take a stand. Most problems, conflicts or situations, don't call for full-blown fights. When someone behaves unreasonably or unfairly, stop for a moment and remember: *you have a choice.*

Often it's better to just back off – especially if a conflict will mean you'll get so upset or focused on "getting even," the process might turn your attitude negative.

Answer this for me, how many times can you go "an eye for an eye" with somebody? After all, after only two times at this, aren't you *both* blind? So, the million-dollar question is, who wins? If your relationship with someone has repeatedly turned your attitude negative, the only way to recapture your positive attitude may be to put some distance between yourself and that person. Jesus says,

Luke 9:5 (NIV)
*"If people do not welcome you, leave their town and **shake the dust off your feet** as a testimony against them."*

I like that! Shake the dust off your feet and keep on trucking. In your personal life, putting distance between yourself and another person or even making a complete withdrawal is tough and in close relationships, it's often impossible. Sometimes in life though, you have got to make a decision to do whatever is necessary for your spiritual and emotional success!

DO YOU NEED AN ATTITUDE ADJUSTMENT?

I know life can be very challenging. I also know you can't be positive all the time. So what do you do when the battles of life break you down? First, make minor, daily adjustments. Meditate on God's Word. Think on those things that are good, true, honest, just, pure, lovely and of good report:

Philippians 4:8 (ESV)

*"Finally, brothers, whatever is **true**, whatever is **honorable**, whatever is **just**, whatever is **pure**, whatever is **lovely**, whatever is **commendable**, if there is any **excellence**, if there is anything worthy of praise, think about these things."*

Take a "chill pill." No, not *literally* but do take a break from life. You don't have to travel anywhere. Just get a change of pace or a change of scenery. It's easy to get into a rut without realizing it. Usually though, it takes action of some kind to recapture a positive attitude. This may sound crazy but of the people I know who have foul, negative and evil attitudes, those people may not even know or *realize* they have such unpleasant ways and dispositions. It helps me to think that way to not only protect myself but also to *not judge them*!

EASY ATTITUDE FIXERS

Simplify your life. Get rid of stuff you don't really need. Give to Goodwill or to a local church or even someone you just pass by on the street. My wife randomly handed someone $10 at a gas station and she was giddy all day! Set the spiritual blessings of giving in operation. Giving and blessing others always turns my attitude around! *Make someone else happy* and watch God open doors to make you happy.

Stop putting off things you need to do. William B. Sprague says, *"Do not wait to strike till the iron is hot; but make it hot by striking."* You must take action now. If you just make the first strike, you release spiritual forces to help you make the next move. Don't put off until tomorrow what you can do today!

De-clutter your group of so called "friends" and spend time with the ones who truly have your best interest at heart. You want to be surrounded by support, not naysayers and prognosticators of gloom and doom.

Keep busy and don't be idle. An idle mind is the Devil's workshop. (Did your Mom tell you that one too?)

Understand that every living human being has problems. Nobody is free from problems. A problem-free life is just an illusion. It is a dangerous deception. Problems are equal opportunity harassers. Again, it depends on *how* you *respond* that determines your attitudinal outcome.

There is always a negative and a positive reaction to every problem. Choose to react positively to any situation where you can. It's not easy but it can be done. For every problem, God's got a solution!

YOUR #1 SUCCESS ASSET

What if you and fifteen of your friends each took a sheet of paper, made up a list of your current problems, put them in a big box, mixed them all up (no names listed), then each person drew a sheet (not your own) from the box...what would you find out?

EVERYBODY'S GOT PROBLEMS

Of course, everybody would end up with a list of problems. Some people would find out their list of problems is *less* than the list of other people and possibly less serious. Knowing this would probably help boost their attitude. Others would discover their problems might be more severe but then would realize *nobody is problem free*; another attitude boost.

What does this mean? It means, despite the number or severity of problems in life (money, relationships, health, work, emotional), *PROBLEMS SHOULD NOT* determine a person's attitude! So, *you* have the ability – especially when you are submitted to God – to have a positive attitude no matter what your circumstances! **That is the attitude of success.**

When Paul and Silas were jailed, the Bible does not say they were screaming and crying. Instead, here is what happened...

Acts 16:23-25 (CEV)
"After they had been badly beaten, they were put in jail and the jailer was told to guard them carefully. 24 The jailer did as he was told. He put them deep inside the jail and chained their feet to

heavy blocks of wood. ²⁵About midnight Paul and Silas were praying and singing praises to God, while the other prisoners listened."

What were they doing? They were praying and singing and later, they were set free!

When Shadrach, Meshach and Abednego went to the fiery furnace, they weren't screaming and crying either...

Daniel 3:19-26 (CEV)

"Nebuchadnezzar's face twisted with anger at the three men. And he ordered the furnace to be heated seven times hotter than usual.²⁰ Next, he commanded some of his strongest soldiers to tie up the men and throw them into the flaming furnace. ²¹⁻²³ The king wanted it done at that very moment. So the soldiers tied up Shadrach, Meshach and Abednego and threw them into the flaming furnace with all of their clothes still on, including their turbans. The fire was so hot that flames leaped out and killed the soldiers. ²⁴ Suddenly the king jumped up and shouted, "Weren't only three men tied up and thrown into the fire?" "Yes, Your Majesty," the people answered. ²⁵ "But I see four men walking around in the fire," the king replied. "None of them is tied up or harmed and the fourth one looks like a god." ²⁶ Nebuchadnezzar went closer to the flaming furnace and said to the three young men, "You servants of the Most High God, come out at once!" They came out."

If God was that kind of strength for them, won't He be that *same* strength for you? Remember, He's no respecter of persons (see Acts 10:34).

Even if new situations were to pile up on top of the one's you already face, don't let it steal your best success asset, *your attitude*. It's the *way* you deal with problems and situations that determines your success in life.

GIVING CHANGES FOUL ATTITUDE

A good attitude is not only for your success, it is also for you to have a positive impact on others. Over the years I have found that giving can change a foul attitude to one that is sweet and joyful. It brings just as much of an attitude boost, if not more, to the giver.

I once worked with a woman who somehow mistakenly got the idea I disliked her; she had a very negative attitude towards me. I had absolutely nothing against the woman but somehow she had gotten the idea that I was her enemy. I would speak to her and she would refuse to speak back or would just grunt instead.

One day, the idea came to me to do something to end this matter. I would try to change her foul attitude to one of success. I decided to buy her the most beautiful green plant; I think it was a peace lily. I planned to give the plant to her early one morning when I came to work. Time slipped away from me and I needed to rush out of the office to get to an appointment on time.

I left the plant with the guard and I asked him to pass it on to my disgruntled co-worker. I told the guard to leave the plant in the lobby and explain to her that I had left the plant for her. When I returned to the office the next day, he shared what happened with the woman and the plant.

He says he told her I left a gift for her and all she had to do was to go to the lobby to get it. He said she looked out into the lobby, turned around, looked at him and said, "Is that for me?" He said, "Yes, that's for you." He said she repeated the question, "That's for me?" in a voice of utter disbelief. He told her again, "Yes!" Again she asked, "*That's for me?*" For the third time he said, "*Yes, it is!*" He told me he could see the light bulb go off and her eyes became bright and her grimace turned to a bright smile.

The guard said the woman became so excited and so uplifted, she immediately took her lunch break and took the plant home. After receiving the plant, that woman's attitude totally changed toward me. I never had to speak first to her again, because *she never gave me the chance*!

"One must learn to make others happy
if one wants to be happy."
-Swedish Proverb

5

SUCCESS THROUGH WORDS

Proverbs 18:21 (GW)
"The tongue has the power of life and death and those who love to talk will have to eat their own words."

Proverbs 18:21 (KJV)
"Death and life are in the power of the tongue: and they that love it shall eat the fruit thereof."

I know at some point, just like you, I have told someone to shut his or her mouth. Were we really telling them just to close their mouth? Of course not! What we were really saying was - **stop talking – I don't want to hear what you are saying!** "The tongue" is used throughout Scripture, in both literal and metaphorical ways; especially in the books of Psalms, Proverbs and James.

The tongue is a small part of the body, yet, as we see in the scriptures above, it has the power of life and death. This holds true whether we're speaking of spiritual, physical or emotional life and death.

WORDS HAVE POWER

"Words are, of course, the most powerful drug used by mankind."
-Rudyard Kipling

For example, take the comment: "The White House issued a statement." Of course, the White House is a building, it can't talk nor can it issue statements. We know that. In this instance, the White House refers to the President, who lives there. Words can mean different things in different situations.

Without giving much thought to the subject, many people would tell you words are *void of power*. They may also say that words do not have a great impact on the hearer. Most of us have held the view that the worst thing words can do is hurt someone's feelings. Much credence has been given to the old cliché, "sticks and stones may break my bones but words will never hurt me."

When the subject of words is carefully considered, I believe that most people would agree words could be used to inflict great harm or bestow great blessings. Unfortunately, most people give very little thought to the power of their words and therefore never place much emphasis on spoken words; be they words that are full of life *or* full of death.

God has a different opinion and attitude about the value and significance of words as seen in the following scripture:

Matthew 12:36-37 (AMP)
"But I tell you, on the day of judgment men will have to give **account for every idle (inoperative, nonworking) word they speak.** *37 For by your words you will be justified and acquitted and by your words you will be condemned and sentenced."*

In this scripture, the Lord is simply saying, your words can be used to help you or your words can be used to hurt you. Accordingly, God does not give credence to the erroneous view that words are insignificant.

NATURAL IMPACT OF WORDS

If the average person would conscientiously and carefully think about the importance and ramifications of spoken words, the person would come to the realization that words are instruments of power, influence and authority. For example, we rely on words in everyday life to make marriage proposals and enter into what is supposed to be a lifetime commitment.

Words such as, "thank you" and "I love you" will positively impact a person and bring happiness and joy to him or her. We also use words to give accolades and bestow recognition for successful endeavors and achievements. To do this, we speak words such as "you did an excellent job" or "congratulations" or "you were wonderful." The utterance of these words will bring pleasure and satisfaction to the hearer.

During natural, everyday living, no responsible parent would want to hear the words, "Your child is going to flunk out of school" even if the statement is untrue. Who wants to hear the words "you're going to get fired!" or "you will never get out of debt?" These words negatively impact the listener even if they are not accurate. It takes many positive words to lift someone up but only one or two negative words to pop their bubble. Just let someone call you stupid! How would *you* react?

Has anyone ever said something negative to you and you just wilted and felt like you were torn apart inside? It's happened to me more times than I care to mention. Or perhaps they said some beautiful words to you and then you just blossomed like a flower. We will be able to tame the tongue with God's help and only speak words of life and success.

~~~~~~~~~~~~~~~~~~~~~
A tongue has no bones but has enough strength to break a heart!
~~~~~~~~~~~

SPIRITUAL IMPACT OF WORDS

From a spiritual standpoint, words can be used to bless or curse as stated in James 3:10. Although people realize that, in the natural, words can be either pleasant or unpleasant, they still do not believe spoken words can produce spiritual consequences, *good or evil*.

The spiritual effect of words can manifest in the natural realm in forms such as sickness, disease, marital discord, prosperity, health, happiness or even death.

The Bible tells us plainly and simply, death and life are in the power of the tongue (Proverbs 18:21). The book of James tells us words can be used to bless or curse (see James 3:10). These scriptures mean someone can speak words on a person's life that can bring good, rewarding and beneficial results. They also mean someone can speak words on a person's life that can bring evil, harm and turbulence.

NEGATIVE WORDS ARE EASY

It often seems that *negative* words are easier to say and can take root much deeper and are far more common. But, that doesn't make it right. Most of us probably beat ourselves up a bit with our own words, from time to time but we shouldn't. Whenever we tell ourselves: I'm so fat, stupid, lazy, ugly, boring or sinful, we are choosing death. That's NOT what God says about us. Anytime we call ourselves names or put ourselves down, we are speaking death over ourselves. Worse still, we are insulting God, who created us in His image and loves us with an everlasting love.

This type of verbal assault isn't only directed inwardly toward ourselves. It often is directed outwardly toward others also.

When we insult others, lie, speak maliciously, or gossip – to or about other people, we are speaking death. We should be ever mindful to control the words we speak, as it says in Proverbs 4:24, "Keep your mouth free of perversity; keep corrupt talk far from your lips" (NIV).

FAVORABLE CONSEQUENCES

There can be a negative impact by words but there can be a positive impact as well. What is most important to us is that which is positive. We have got to use words that produce life and success. It is good to know about the dark side of life so we can stand against the wiles of evil but it is so much better to live and have our being in the positive (the side of light and life). There are many scriptures that support the view that words can produce life, blessings and material rewards.

Genesis 1 tells us God created the universe by speaking words such as, "Let there be light." God used words to bring into physical existence, those things He desired. In the same chapter, we see God used words to bless the living creatures He created. His words were, "Be fruitful and multiply and fill the waters in the seas and let fowl multiply in the earth" (Genesis 1:22).

WORDS CAN BLESS

In Genesis 12, we see that God blessed Abraham with spoken

words by saying, "I will bless thee and make thy name great; and thou shalt be a blessing" (Genesis 12:2). Abraham was richly and enormously blessed. He was made the father of many nations, given vast amounts of land and was very rich in cattle, silver and gold (see Genesis 13:2).

In the book of Acts, we see many instances in which the spoken word was used to bring blessings. For instance, spoken words were used by Peter to bring healing to a man who had been lame from his mother's womb (see Acts 3:2–8). This obviously was a blessing to a man who had been lame all of his life. What is more important is that spoken words were used to preach the gospel and get thousands of people saved (Acts 2:40–41) and to raise people from the dead (Acts 9:37–41).

Salvation and the new birth are both received by confessing Jesus with your mouth and believing that God raised Him from the dead (see Romans 10:9). Words are spoken to receive the gift of eternal life. Words can be used to produce life, prosperity, healing and magnificent blessings.

WORDS CAN CURSE

The Bible teaches us that words can be used to bring negative consequences (James 3:10). One of the clearest examples of how words can bring a curse is seen in:

Mark 11:13–14, 20-21 (GW)
*"In the distance he saw a fig tree with leaves. He went to see if he could find any figs on it. When he came to it, he found nothing but leaves because it wasn't the season for figs. ¹⁴ Then he said to the tree, **"No one will ever eat fruit from you again!"** His disciples heard this."..."While Jesus and his disciples were walking early in the morning, they saw that the fig tree had dried up. ²¹ Peter remembered what Jesus had said, so he said to Jesus, "Rabbi, look! **The fig tree you cursed has dried up.**"*

Jesus cursed a fig tree and it withered away as a result of His spoken words. Another example of a curse that came as a result of spoken words is found in Genesis 27. Rebecca placed a curse on herself. Jacob, her son, said he would be cursed because he deceived his father, Isaac. Rebecca placed the curse on herself:

Genesis 27:13 (GW)
*"His mother responded, "**Let any curse on you fall on me**, Son. Just obey me and go! Get me the young goats."*

The curse was placed upon her life by her own words. The Bible says, "by our words we are justified and by our words we are condemned" (Matthew 12:37).

HEROD

Acts 12:21-23 (GW)
"The appointed day came. Herod, wearing his royal clothes, sat on his throne and began making a speech to them. ²² The people started shouting, "The voice of a god and not of a man!" ²³ Immediately, an angel from the Lord killed Herod for not giving

*glory to God. **Herod was eaten by maggots and he died.***"

Here we learn that Herod's words, as well as the words of the people in his presence, apparently brought great displeasure to God. Herod gave a very persuasive speech to the people. They shouted and said his voice was that of a god and not a man. He did not give God the appropriate recognition and glory.

Instead, he claimed all the glory for himself. As a result, the Lord poured out His wrath. The angel of the Lord killed Herod...and he was eaten by maggots and died. The spoken words of these individuals cost Herod to lose his life. As you can see, death and life are truly in the power of the tongue.

ANANIAS AND SAPPHIRA

Acts 5:1-11 (CEV)

*"Ananias and his wife Sapphira also sold a piece of property. [2] But **they agreed to cheat** and keep some of the money for themselves. So when Ananias took the rest of the money to the apostles, [3] Peter said,"Why has Satan made you keep back some of the money from the sale of the property? Why have **you lied to the Holy Spirit?** [4] The property was yours before you sold it and even after you sold it, the money was still yours. What made you do such a thing? You didn't lie to people. **You lied to God!**" [5] As soon as Ananias heard this, he dropped dead and everyone who heard about it was frightened. [6] Some young men came in and wrapped up his body. Then they took it out and buried it. [7] Three hours later Sapphira came in but she did not know what had happened to her husband. [8] Peter asked her, "Tell me, did you sell the property for this*

*amount?" "Yes," she answered, "that's the amount." ⁹ Then Peter said, "Why did the two of you agree to test the Lord's Spirit? The men who buried Ananias are by the door and they will carry you out!" ¹⁰ At **once she fell at Peter's feet and died**. When the young men came back in, they found Sapphira lying there dead. So they carried her out and buried her beside her husband. ¹¹ The church members were afraid and so was everyone else who heard what had happened."*

Their spoken words caused them to lose their lives!

THE CHILDREN OF ISRAEL

Perhaps the best example in the Bible of how words can cause death is in this scripture...

Numbers 14:1-4 (GW)

*"Then all the people in the Israelite community raised their voices and cried out loud all that night. ² They **complained** to Moses and Aaron, "If only we had died in Egypt or this desert! ³ Why is the Lord bringing us to this land—just to have us die in battle? Our wives and children will be taken as prisoners of war! Wouldn't it be better for us to go back to Egypt?" ⁴ They said to each other, "**Let's choose a leader and go back to Egypt.**"*

The children of Israel complained against God, Moses and Aaron. Although God had taken them out of Egypt, freeing them of bondage, they complained and said the conditions in Egypt were better than the conditions in the wilderness. These verses reveal that the Israelites murmured a great deal. To murmur means to gripe, criticize or complain. Despite all the miraculous things God had done for them, they still grumbled, griped and complained! The essence of what the Israelites said was they were dissatisfied with the conditions and wished they had died in Egypt or the desert. There are at least three reasons why the complaints and murmurings of the Israelites brought on their destruction.

1. By **complaining** against Moses and Aaron, they touched God's anointed. The Bible clearly says, "Touch not mine anointed and do my prophets no harm" (Psalms 105:15). Moses and Aaron were God's anointed. By complaining against Moses and Aaron, the children of Israel "touched" or spoke evil of God's anointed and displeased God.

2. By **murmuring,** the Israelites gave God another reason to be dissatisfied. The grumbling amounted to rebellion. God hates rebellion. Rebellion vexes the Holy Spirit (Isaiah 63:10). Furthermore, rebellion is as the sin of witchcraft. The Bible tells us that witchcraft is an abomination (something God hates or detests) in the eyes of God (Deuteronomy 18:9-12). For this additional reason, God disapproved of the murmuring by the Israelites.

3. By **grumbling** and stating they wished they were dead, the Israelites spoke death and destruction upon themselves. This is how the Lord responded to their grumblings:

Numbers 14:26-29 (GW)
"Then the Lord said to Moses and Aaron, [27]"How long must I put up with this wicked community that keeps complaining about me? I've heard the complaints the Israelites are making about me. [28] So

tell them, 'As I live, declares the Lord, I solemnly swear I will do everything to you that you said I would do. [29] **Your bodies will drop dead in this desert. All of you who are at least 20 years old, who were registered and listed and who complained about me will die."**

God told them, *what you say is what you get.* You said you would die; so death you will receive. This is a vivid illustration of how death was produced as a result of spoken words. Death and life are truly in the power of the tongue (Proverbs 18:21). The Israelites wished for death and said they were going to experience death. As a result, they received death (Numbers 14:29–45).

OUR WORDS MOVE JESUS

Jesus Christ is the Apostle and High Priest of our confession (Hebrews 3:1). Jesus is also our Advocate (1 John 2:1), who sits at the right hand of God the Father where he ever sits to make intercession for us (Hebrews 7:25). Jesus also serves as our High Priest (Hebrews 8:1). A High Priest is one who intercedes for others and represents them before God. Jesus acts as a Mediator or on our behalf (Hebrews 8:6).

When we start speaking God's Word over and over, it is not logical to think our High Priest and Intercessor remains silent. Our Intercessor and High Priest speaks to the father and intercedes for us. This is because the Bible tells us *one* of the roles of Jesus is to serve as High Priest of our profession or confession (what we say). Jesus can be moved to intercede for us based on the words that *we* speak!

SPEAK WORDS OF LIFE

As we have seen, death and life are in the power of the tongue (see Proverbs 18:21). Instead of speaking evil words that produce death and negative consequences, speak words of life and success. Words from scripture, as well as words that are consistent with scripture, produce fruit and life. Agree with God and speak health, life and success into your life and environment.

Jesus, in John 6:63 said, "It is the Spirit that quickeneth; the flesh profiteth nothing: the words that I speak unto you, they are Spirit and they are life." Do you see it? The flesh profits nothing. The flesh is the carnal mind. Speak words of life and prepare to receive victory and success.

REMEMBER

Speak the Word of God several times a day, everyday to reprogram your mind with success. The greater the needs in your life are, the more you need God's Word working for you. Allow God's Word to feed your spirit and give the Word an opportunity to sink in your spirit! Fight the good fight of faith. *Don't* give up on the Word. *Never* give up on the Word.

No one should do more for you than you would do for yourself. You hold the ability to change your life through the Word of God. Make God's Word an integral part of your life. Speak faith filled words boldly, courageously, diligently and relentlessly.

Joshua 1:8 (GW)
*"**Never stop reciting these teachings**. You must think about them night and day so that you will faithfully do everything written in them. **Only then will you prosper and succeed.**"*

"Remember not only to say the right thing in the right place, but far more difficult still, to leave unsaid the wrong thing at the tempting moment."
— Benjamin Franklin

6

SUCCESS THROUGH GODLINESS

"Every young man would do well to remember that all successful business stands on the foundation of morality."
-Henry Ward Beecher

I'm always talking to people about living godly lives. The main question I get is, "What is godliness?" My simple answer is that godliness means having a character that conforms to the laws and wishes of God, as expressed in the Bible.

"The chief factor in any man's success or failure
must be his own character."
– Theodore Roosevelt

The words godly and godliness appear only a few times in the New Testament, yet the entire Bible is a book on godliness.

Titus 2:11-13 (ESV)
*"For the grace of God has appeared, bringing salvation for all people, [12] training us to renounce ungodliness and worldly passions and to **live self-controlled, upright and godly lives** in the present age, [13] waiting for our blessed hope, the appearing of the glory of our great God and Savior Jesus Christ."*

WHAT'S GOOD ABOUT BELIEVING IN JESUS?

By believing in Jesus, you receive salvation and the gift of eternal life. This is the *greatest blessing* from God. As great as salvation is, there are many *other* rewards that we are capable of receiving as a result of following Jesus.

What are those rewards? The answer lies in a number of scriptures. The scripture that may best describe the numerous rewards, blessings and benefits of serving God is, 1 Timothy 4:8, "but godliness is profitable unto all things, having promise of the life that now is and of that which is to come." This scripture is brief but it is loaded.

It means that not only has God arranged for us to have the great blessing of eternal life but while we are here on earth, we have the potential to be successful *at all we do*. This means that God will help us succeed and do well in every area of life that relates to good and godly matters.

STEPS TO SUCCESS

Since God has promised us we will profit in all ways (be successful), we need to know how to take advantage of this wonderful blessing. To achieve in life, we must understand that certain conditions must be met to obtain the success God has promised us. After coming to the Lord, we must start to live according to the biblical rules of God.

Clearly, we must obey the Ten Commandments but we should avoid becoming excessively sin conscious. When you continually say to yourself, "I must not sin," this produces the negative result of making you focus on sin. Whatever you focus on, either good or bad, the thing you focus on, will come upon you. This, I believe is what happened to Job.

Even people who don't know much about the Bible know about the suffering of Job. Let's look at one of the main reasons Job went through so much suffering. Job said, "The thing which I greatly feared is come upon me" (Job 3:25 KJV).

WHAT YOU FOCUS ON IS WHAT YOU GET

It takes a great deal of skill for high wire walkers to safely walk the high wire. During their training, high wire walkers are told they should never look down. If they look down, they will fall off the wire and have very tragic results.

Similarly, racecar drivers are trained to avoid looking at the wall that surrounds the racetrack. If they look too much at the wall, they will drive into it. Police officers are taught, when pulling over a car for speeding or some other reason, they must be very careful. One reason is that when passing motorists see the flashing lights on the police car, they get fixated or focused on the flashing lights. Strangely, the flashing lights tend to draw the passing motorists right into the police car; often causing serious accidents. They often drive into the very vehicle (the police car) they would *never*, in a million years, want to drive into!

The lesson is to always focus on the positive. By way of comparison, we must always focus on God and righteous living instead of focusing on avoiding failure, sin and evil. We should follow the wise counsel of Philippians 4:8 which says, think on those things that are true, honest, just, pure, lovely and of good report. Why? What you focus on is what you get!

REASONS FOR OBEYING GOD'S WORD

In the field of law, we use an expression or maxim that says, *"the law of equity does not require an idle gesture."* This means the law of equity will not require a person do something that has no worth or importance.

~~~~~~~~~~~~~~~~~~~

Clearly, if the law will not require the doing of a useless act, then certainly God would not place any requirements on us that have no value.

~~~~~~~~~~~

If God says we are supposed to obey His Word, then it is important that we do so. The book of James tells us we must be "doers of the word and not hearers only" (James 1:22). The scripture goes on to say, if you do what God's Word says and don't forget it, *then* you will be blessed in your deeds or blessed for doing His Word (James 1:25). There are negative consequences for disobeying the Word of God but remember we must focus on the positive and not the negative. We get blessings and rewards for obeying God's Word. This is the beginning of true success.

BEING FILLED WITH THE HOLY SPIRIT

When we as Believers get filled with the Holy Spirit, we possess and display the fruit of the Spirit of God who lives in us. The fruit of the Spirit is love, joy, peace, patience, goodness, kindness, gentleness, faithfulness and self-control (Galatians 5:22-23 NIV).

The Holy Spirit gives us knowledge to know what to do and where to turn (Proverbs 3:5-6), wisdom (James 1:5) and the peace of God that passes all understanding (Philippians 4:7). As we grow and mature in the Holy Spirit, we begin *to think not only of ourselves but of others as well.* My greatest joy, in life right now, is finding out what I can do for people, how my wife and I can help them grow and prosper spiritually, physically, socially, emotionally and financially.

I am fully aware and knowledgeable that a person can have all the power, money, popularity and prestige the world has to offer but if his or her soul is empty and bitter, worldly success is really *failure*.

"For what is a man profited, if he shall gain the whole world and lose his own soul? or what shall a man give in exchange for his soul?"

GODLY LIVING

I grew up in a small, central Texas community called Tomlinson Hill. And even as a child, I noticed the needs were *always* very great there. This instilled in me the desire to progress in life and do something to help my family and other people. I didn't know one of the main ways to help others was through prayer and sharing with them the gospel of Jesus Christ.

Even beyond Tomlinson Hill, I noticed that people in the area needed cars, homes, jobs, good health, education and legal help. I used to think prayer only worked every now and then. I thought the gospel was mainly just the method God used to get people to heaven.

"You can no more blame your circumstances for your character than you can blame the mirror for the way you look."
-Anonymous

GODLINESS IS A GOOD LIFE

I thought that it was only evil and ungodly people who got ahead in life. I believed that while on earth, Believers just naturally had to suffer and they would get their blessings and rewards in heaven. To a limited extent, this is true. Yes, there will be rewards in heaven and yes there will be troubles on earth.

I didn't know that Believers could get rewards and be successful and victorious on earth. I didn't know that, according to scripture, God rewards those who diligently seek Him (Hebrews 11:6). This means people will be rewarded here on earth if they diligently seek God.

I didn't know that the Bible says when we pray, our requests would be answered if we believe (Mark 11:24). I didn't know that God would supply all our needs, here on earth, through Christ Jesus according to Philippians 4:19.

As we go through troubles and hard times – which the Bible calls "trials" – we are able to endure with great peace and direction; we begin to understand that God uses those very trials to benefit us (John 16:33; James 1:2).

In other words, trouble in life is not intended to *cause* us to *fail*. It is intended for us to walk through trouble with God's grace and wisdom. By obeying God, we gain freedom from the curses of this world—hate, jealousy, addictions, confusion, inferiority complexes, sadness without reason, anger, bitterness, unforgiveness, selfishness and more.

~~~~~~~~~~~~~~~~~~~~~~

It is a life of loving and following God that writes the blueprint for our path of success. Whatever you want, in life, can only be fully experienced and enjoyed by living a godly life!

~~~~~~~~~~~

"Do all the good you can. By all the means you can.
In all the ways you can. In all the places you can.
At all the times you can. To all the people you can.
As long as ever you can."
— John Wesley

7

SUCCESS THROUGH SPIRITUAL WEAPONS

2 Corinthians 10:4 (ESV)
*"For the weapons of our warfare are not of the flesh but have **divine power** to destroy strongholds."*

The Word of the Lord tells us His thoughts are not our thoughts and His ways are not our ways (Isaiah 55:8). The scripture goes on to tell us that as the heavens are higher than the earth, so are God's ways higher than our ways (see Isaiah 55:9). Because God's ways are different from our ways, He has given us spiritual weapons to fight our battles.

The Bible states it this way: "for the weapons our warfare are not carnal but mighty through God to the pulling down of strongholds" (2 Corinthians 10:4). This means we use spiritual weapons to defeat and overcome evil and bondage.

~~~~~~~~~~~~~~~~~~~~

As a Believer in Jesus Christ, you must thoroughly understand the power of God is with you, to destroy the power of the enemy against you.

~~~~~~~~~~~

For instance, when we get angry with someone, we as Believers are not supposed to use a gun or knife to settle the dispute. Rather, we are supposed to use prayer, forgiveness, wisdom, love and understanding to resolve the problem. God has given us many other spiritual weapons such as the name of Jesus, the quotation of scripture, prayer, praise, fasting, wisdom and giving.

THE NAME OF JESUS

Proverbs 18:10 (ESV)
"The name of the Lord is a strong tower;
the righteous man runs into it and is safe."

One of the most powerful weapons we have is the name of the Lord Jesus. Let's return to the forward of this book to see a great example of how the name of Jesus was used to work wonders. It reads: "In all my years of being at a hospital, I have never, ever seen doctors or nurses so panicked. I knew I had to call Apostle Washington. So I called him right away to advise him of what was going on.

"He quickly said, "Let's pray and put your wife on speaker phone." I did so immediately. *I will never forget this as long as I live.* He specifically said, "George, you *must* place your hand on your wife's abdomen (on the baby) before we pray." When I had my hands in place, he began to pray; but this prayer was different from his usual methods of praying. He began to shout, "Jesus, Jesus, Jesus, Jesus!

"That was the entirety of the prayer, for about ten minutes! My son's heart rate had been dropping fast and my wife was in excruciating pain. Apostle kept saying repeatedly, "Jesus, Jesus, Jesus." It began to sound like a shouting cry. Suddenly, my son's heart rate began to increase! Finally, his heartbeat became normal!" The Bible tells us the name of Jesus is above *every* name (see Philippians 2:9). His name is greater than any problem or sickness. I used this name to conquer trouble during the delivery of my friend's child.

THE MOST WIDELY USED WEAPON

Even before I became a Believer, I had seen the success of prayer as it worked wonders for my family. My mother was a soft-spoken, dedicated, very strong, "sold out to Jesus" Believer, who would daily lift up prayers for the family. I know those prayers sustained my family and kept me out of trouble.

I vividly remember an incident that took place when I was in college. An accident occurred that almost claimed the life of my father. My brother, Lawrence, called me at Prairie View A&M, where I was attending college. He told me our father had been seriously injured on the job and that his neck had been broken. He went on to say our dad was paralyzed and was in the intensive care unit of the hospital in Temple, Texas. He further said that the doctors told them that our father *might not ever walk again*. Not only did I become speechless and breathless at this news, I felt more helpless than I had ever felt in my entire life. As my brother continued to speak, I found it very hard to hold back the tears. My father was such a lively, outgoing, friendly and loving person that it was very painful to think of him spending the rest of his life in a wheel chair.

MY MOTHER THE PRAYER WARRIOR

My mother worked across town from the hospital where my father was being treated. She said she went to the hospital and found that our father could not move his hands or legs. After my mother left the hospital, she went into prayer action; she may have even started fasting too! She told me she asked God to heal and restore my father to health. Within a very short time, about one hour, my father began to move one of his legs.

A short time later, my father moved the other leg. Later on, his health was restored and he became able to walk and function in a normal manner. The prayer of my mother, Alma Inez Washington, worked wonders as God moved powerfully to free my father from paralysis.

EFFECTUAL FERVENT PRAYER

After coming to the Lord, I learned how to pray for myself, as well as pray and intercede for others. I learned that the "effectual fervent prayer of a righteous man availeth much"

(James 5:16). This means that you have to pray strongly and forcefully to get the results you desire. It should be noted that righteous living is necessary to get your prayers successfully answered.

What is righteous living? Be truthful, treat others fairly, obey the law and act as though Jesus is standing there with you and watching every action you take. Again, the scripture shows us it's good to follow or obey the Word of God. Remember to focus on the positive and righteous, rather than focus on the evil and unrighteous.

MILITARY METHODS MIRRORED

After years of doing a great deal of research and studying the Bible, I found that God often likes us to use several spiritual weapons at one time when we're trying to succeed and overcome the challenges of life. He provides greater blessings when two or more spiritual weapons are combined instead of using the weapons separately or individually.

Then, I learned that in the secular world we have followed the example of God when coming against certain problems. Let's look at our military for example. Instead of relying totally on ground soldiers with military rifles, during war, the army also uses tanks, artillery, helicopters and many other weapons.

By combining all these weapons, our military is made much

stronger than it would be using only infantry soldiers with rifles. Our local police forces have found that, instead of relying totally on the police officer with a handgun, it is sometimes better to use the SWAT team with rifles and other weapons.

THE COMBINATION OF WEAPONS

In the medical field, it has been found that when two medications are combined, this sometimes produces more power and more effective results. The scripture says it this way: "**two are better than one** for they have a good reward for their labour" (Ecclesiastes 4:9).

This means when resources are combined, there is unity. The combination of the two will produce much greater results than the individuals working separately. This idea of combining resources to obtain greater results can be seen in the book of Matthew.

Specifically, in the King James version of the Bible, the scripture says, "If two of you shall agree on earth as touching anything that they shall ask, it shall be done for them of my Father which is in heaven"(Matthew 18:19). This means, if two people on Earth agree concerning anything they ask God the Father to do, then He will bless the prayers of two or more people praying in harmony and unity lifted up to Him.

The benefit of combining resources can easily be seen in situations like a family reunion. Many times I have seen clubs, church groups and family members join forces successfully for a common purpose. Each individual of a group has agreed to bring a "covered dish" to celebrate some occasion. The result is, by combining resources; people can have a great big feast instead of two or three getting together and just bringing, bread, meat and drinks!

PRAYER AND FASTING

Isaiah 58:6 (NIV)
*"Is not this the kind of fasting I have chosen: to loose the chains of injustice and untie the cords of the yoke, to **set the oppressed free** and break every yoke?"*

As we have seen, prayer by itself can bring great, wondrous, amazing and miraculous results. Fasting alone can also produce results but, when fasting and prayer are combined, the results are far greater than when using these weapons individually or separately.

A friend of mine once told me he lent someone a large sum of money (thousands of dollars) and the borrower refused to pay back the loan. After two years had passed the borrower still had not paid the loan. My friend said because he had not gotten his money back after two years, he decided to pray and fast for five days.

He said on the fifth day, God did a great and mighty work. My friend told me on day number five, the borrower called and said, "Hey, I got your money!" To his amazement, the loan was paid off. My friend had gotten his money as the direct result of prayer and fasting.

WHEN A MAN FINDS A WIFE

"A man without a wife is like a vase without flowers."
-African Proverb

After I came to the Lord, I told my mother I didn't want to have anything to do with marriage. My mother said, "Son you're now a saved man and you need to have a good wife." My mother knew that the Bible says that when a man finds a wife, he has found a good thing and he gets favor from God (Proverbs 18:22).

I listened to her and thought carefully about what she said. Then I asked my mother if she would pray for me to get a good and righteous wife. She immediately told me she would. My mother has gone on to be with the Lord but she was one godly woman!

I asked my mother what the secret was to her spiritual success and closeness to God. She told me the secret to her success was that each and every week of her life she prayed often and she fasted at least two days out of every week!

My mother prayed for me to get a good wife and shortly after her prayer, I had a very vivid dream about a woman holding the hand of a little girl. A month or so later, I agreed to be a part of a good friend's wedding in another city. At that wedding I saw a woman who resembled the woman in the vivid dream. She told me her name was Nicole and that she was attending graduate school.

I started talking to her and we talked on and on. She lived in Atlanta and I lived in San Antonio. We exchanged telephone numbers and talked to each other on the phone every day. I then went on a thirty day fast skipping breakfast and lunch each day. After fasting and praying for about twenty days, something happened that changed my life. While on my knees praying and praising God, the Lord impressed on my mind that Nicole was the woman He had sent to me, to be my wife.

I then realized and discerned Nicole was the woman I had seen in the dream. My mother had prayed and fasted and I had prayed and fasted. The result was that *I met the person who would become my wife.*

FEAR SETS IN

After receiving the revelation that Nicole was to be my wife, I finally got the courage to propose to her. She agreed to marry me! Excited, I immediately started telling people I was engaged. Sometimes when you share your good news with others, it is bad news to them. When I started sharing my great news, people started praying strange prayers and I started having weird feelings about the marriage.

EVERYBODY IS NOT HAPPY FOR YOU

We should always be aware that prayer should never be used to try to violate or go against a person's free will. About the same time I became engaged to Nicole, I felt led to move my membership from one church to another. Both churches were good but I felt led to move on.

One day as I was out and about, I ran into a woman who was a member of my prior church. She said, "Brother, we have been praying for you." I responded, "What have you all been praying?" She said, "We've been praying for you to come back to our church." I thought to myself, "I'm trying to leave and they're trying to pray me back to a church where I don't feel called to stay any longer."

Think about it! Shouldn't I have been able to use my free will to attend church and worship where I felt God wanted me? I was very displeased! We should *never* pray negative prayers asking that negative conditions come upon a person with whom we disagree or dislike. Each day I felt as though I was in a fog. God only knows what kinds of negative and ungodly prayers and words were spoken regarding my engagement.

CAN'T OVERRIDE SOMEONE'S FREE WILL

The Lord does not answer prayers spoken to harm people or override their free will. It's not right to pray something like, "God cause John to have a bad wreck to make him stop driving so fast." The righteous way to pray would be to say something like, "Lord, John drives too fast so I ask that You open his eyes to show him the error of his ways."

Then say, "Move on his heart to persuade him to obey the law and drive properly, in the name of Jesus." In my case, I don't know exactly what was being said or prayed. All I know is that before the engagement was announced I felt great but after it was announced, I felt miserable.

WORDS BRING DEATH AND LIFE

To make matters even worse, one woman who claimed to get valid words and messages from God came to me after church one day to "set me straight." She said God told her I was making a big mistake. The woman boldly told me to my face I had picked the wrong woman to be my wife. She was insinuating that my marriage was going to bring me misery, suffering and pain.

> **"Only he that has travelled the road**
> **knows where the holes are deep."**
> **-Chinese Proverb**

I was new to Christianity and this woman had been in church a great deal longer than I had. The words she spoke to me were chilling. Her words made me *very* nervous. According to Proverbs 18:21, death and life are in the power of the tongue (see chapter 5 for more on this subject). I felt very disappointed by these stinging and discouraging words. Then I remembered my mother had prayed for me to get a good wife. I kept thinking about what my mother had done.

I continually thought about the vivid dream and the revelation I had gotten from God about Nicole being my wife after praying and fasting for twenty days. At the same time, I kept thinking about the horrifying words the woman in church had spoken to me.

IGNORANCE IS NOT BLISS

"Fall seven times and stand up eight."
–Japanese Proverb

At that point in my life I didn't know much about the Bible but I did know the Bible says, "God is *not* the author of confusion but of peace" (1 Corinthians 14:33). I was confused and I had no peace. I was very worried and overcome by fear. Something was terribly wrong! If God is not the author of confusion, then guess who is! The enemy *is* the author of confusion, worry and trouble. God does not answer negative and ungodly prayers but guess who does! It's the enemy.

I didn't know much but I did have the wisdom to seek help from one of the ministers at the church. The minister told me negative and ungodly prayers and words had victimized me. He laid his hand on my head and prayed for me. Amazingly, the fear, worry, stress and confusion immediately disappeared. Never in my life had I had such an experience!

I felt like I could have gone out to run in the world's longest marathon or climb Mount Everest (the highest mountain in the world). I felt as though someone had removed 500 pounds off my shoulders. The joy of the Lord had come upon me and I never again had any worry or fear about getting married.

I proposed to Nicole, she accepted! Shortly before we got married, I prayed and went on a three day fast to ensure our wedding would be problem free. My fasting and praying proved beneficial, as our wedding was very successful!

JOB PROBLEM SOLVED BY FASTING

I have personally seen God work through fasting to bring happiness, joy and freedom in my life on a great number of occasions. One time, when I supervised attorneys years ago, I was facing a very serious office inspection and I was relatively new to the job. The inspection involved reviewing our lawsuits, office procedures and all of our office records. Because I was so new to the job, I felt I had not had sufficient time to prepare to do well on the inspection.

The office simply was not ready for an inspection. We had a very heavy caseload consisting of many lawsuits and other work. We were overburdened and very stressed.

NATURAL SKILLS NEED HELP

I knew I could not handle the problems using my natural abilities. So I turned to prayer and fasting and asked the Lord to postpone the inspection until my staff and I could properly prepare. The Lord answered the prayer and the inspection was postponed. Shortly after that hurdle was overcome, a new inspection was scheduled. Again, I went into fasting and prayer and the inspection was delayed for the second time.

The inspectors then scheduled the inspection for the third time. I still did not feel my staff and I could properly handle an inspection. By now, I suppose you can predict, without me telling you, what I did. Yet again, I depended on prayer and fasting. I asked the Lord to delay or stop the inspection. Again, the inspection was postponed.

By this time the inspection officials had become uneasy about scheduling the inspection for the fourth time. One of the inspectors felt that all the postponements might be some kind of "sign" that the inspection should not take place. Of course, I was still fasting on and off. The inspection was scheduled for the fourth time and the Lord allowed this inspection to take place. Knowing the inspection would be challenging and stressful, I asked the Lord to give me the knowledge, wisdom and strength to see me through this burdensome ordeal.

The inspectors who came into the office had searched the records and found some of our office notes. The notes showed that no one on the legal staff had an answer to an important legal question.

The inspectors, in essence said, "It's now been months since you were puzzled by the legal question of how to handle this case." The preparation for the inspection involved so much work; I was unable to read every note in every case. The inspectors essentially said, "Okay Mr. Supervisor, what's your answer now after all these months have gone by?"

GOD IS ON TIME

I briefly paused and all of a sudden, as if God Himself took over my mouth, *I heard the answer I was giving them and was astonished and amazed!* I even cited the number and name of the proper legal regulation that was supposed to be used to fix the problem! Of course, it was not truly I, it was information given to me by divine revelation! The inspectors looked astonished (don't forget, I was too). I was so happy I felt like shouting right there in the office. I was able to safely survive the inspection.

CONFIDENCE IN GOD

I consider myself to be a *highly confident* person. I realized quickly, in the situations I have described here, I needed *more confidence in God*. The Bible is filled with examples of spiritual battles people have had through the ages. Some have been won some have been lost.

We have to study the Bible to learn the "how to" of winning the battles that face us. I found out how deeply I had to rely on God and His principles of success.

"Suggestions for Fasting and Feasting:
Fast from discontent; feast on thankfulness.
Fast from worry; feast on trust.
Fast from anger; feast on patience.
Fast from self-concern; feast on compassion for others.
Fast from unrelenting pressures; feast on unceasing prayers.
Fast from bitterness; feast on forgiveness.
Fast from discouragement, feast on hope.
Fast from media hype, feast on the honesty of the Bible.
Fast from idle gossip; feast on purposeful silence.
Fast from problems that overwhelm;
feast on prayer that undergirds."
-Anonymous

8

SUCCESS THROUGH GIVING

"Do what you can, where you are, with what you have."
–Teddy Roosevelt

Proverbs 11:25 (CEV)
"Generosity will be rewarded: **Give** *a cup of water,*
and you will **receive** *a cup of water in return."*

Proverbs 28:27 (NIV)
"Those who **give** *to the poor will* **lack nothing** *but those who close*
their eyes to them receive many curses."

Happiness fuels success and giving fuels happiness. Care for others and be a generous giver. Be good to other people. The suffering, death, burial and resurrection of Jesus occurred so those who believe in Him could have eternal life.

GOD WANTS US TO PROSPER

3 John 2 (KJV)
"Beloved, I wish above all things that thou mayest **prosper**
and be in health, even as thy soul prospereth."

This was a desire by the Apostle John. In writing this scripture, John would not make a statement that was inconsistent with the will of God.

Clearly, the Word would not contain a desire that ran counter to the will of God, nor would John make a statement that did not line up with the Word of God. Moreover, John wrote this verse under the inspiration of the Holy Spirit. All Scripture is inspired by God as stated in 2 Timothy 3:16. We can conclude from the scripture, that God wants us to prosper! Further proof that God wants us to prosper can be found in 2 Corinthians 8:9; *"For ye know the grace of our Lord Jesus Christ, that, though he was rich, yet for your sakes he became poor, that ye through his poverty might be rich."*

Many argue the word "riches," as used in this scripture, pertains only to spiritual wealth and not material wealth. This argument cannot be valid because chapter 8 of 2 Corinthians relates to the idea of giving and how *giving results in blessings to the giver and the recipient.*

2 Corinthians 8:1-7(CEV)

*"My friends, we want you to know that the churches in Macedonia have shown others how kind God is. ² Although they were going through hard times and were very poor, they were **glad to give generously**. ³ They gave as much as they could afford and even more, simply because they wanted to. ⁴ They even asked and begged us to let them have the joy of giving their money for God's people. ⁵ And they did more than we had hoped. They gave themselves first to the Lord and then to us, just as God wanted them to do. ⁶ Titus was the one who got you*

*started doing this good thing, so we begged him to have you finish what you had begun. 7 You do everything better than anyone else. You have stronger faith. You speak better and know more. **You are eager to give** and you love us better. **Now you must give more generously than anyone else.**"*

In verses 1 through 7, the Apostle Paul is referring to the giving that was done by the Macedonian churches, *even though* they were in poverty. He pointed out that the people in the Macedonian churches had given most generously. Moreover, it would be incongruous for the Apostle Paul to engage in a discussion about money and giving in verses 1-7 and thereafter confine his discussion to spiritual matters only, in verse 8.

This chapter obviously talks about monetary giving. The substitutionary work of Jesus entitles us to material riches. Jesus explained that He came so that we may have life and have it more abundantly (John 10:10). This abundance, among other things, will enable us to give to help others.

In Ephesians 4:28 (AMP), the word says:
*"Let the thief steal no more but rather let him be industrious, making an honest living with his own hands, so that he may be able to **give to those in need.**"*

As a result, we should earn or obtain money so that others in need can be helped from this abundance. This is further evidence that God wants us to prosper. Additional evidence that God wants us to prosper can be found in several other scriptures.

Psalm 1:1-3 (AMP)
*"**Blessed (happy, fortunate, prosperous and enviable)** is the man who walks and lives not in the counsel of the ungodly [following their advice, their plans and purposes], nor stands [submissive and inactive] in the path where sinners walk, nor sits down [to relax and rest] where the scornful [and the mockers] gather. ²But His law (the precepts, the instructions, the teachings of God) he **habitually meditates (ponders and studies)** by day and by night. ³And he shall be like a tree firmly planted [and tended] by the streams of water, ready to bring forth its fruit in its season; its leaf also shall not fade or wither; and **everything he does shall prosper** [and come to maturity]."*

God desires that we prosper. He would not have told us that we would prosper if we meet the criteria set forth in Psalm 1, if He did not want us to do so! We can take comfort in knowing that God wants us to be blessed, not only spiritually but also materially and financially.

GOD WANTS US TO GIVE

The work of Jesus on Calvary was substitutionary. Along with enabling us to receive eternal life, the redemptive work of Jesus was done so that we might have rewarding, successful and fulfilling lives while here on earth. The Word says, Jesus came so that we may have life and have it more abundantly (see John 10:10). As I have mentioned before, God has given us many spiritual tools to help us excel, and *win in life!*

One of the greatest weapons that we have available to us is giving. Giving is very closely connected to love. God used the tools of love and giving to redeem us and make it possible for us to have eternal life. The very well known scripture that has been used over the years to get people saved mentions these two powerful tools.

That scripture is John 3:16, which says, "For God so loved the world, that He gave His only begotten Son, that whosoever believeth in Him should not perish but have everlasting life." God sent Jesus as a sacrificial gift to redeem us from sin, darkness, evil and bondage. The scripture also says,

Luke 6:38 (CEV)
*"If you give to others, you will be given a full amount in return. It will be packed down, shaken together and spilling over into your lap. **The way you treat others is the way you will be treated**."*

GIVING BRINGS JOY

**"Certain things catch your eye,
but pursue only those that capture the heart."
-Ancient Indian Proverb**

Years ago, I noticed that a 14 year old girl who attended my church, never wore a coat, even when the weather was very cold. I asked a church member why this child never wore a coat. The church member knew the family well and explained that the family was having great financial problems and didn't have enough money to buy the child a coat.

I went to the store, bought a coat and placed it in the hands of the girl's mother to give to her daughter before church. The girl asked her mother, "Why is he doing this?" Over and over she asked, "Why is he doing this?" She apparently found it hard to believe I was only trying to do the will of God. The girl obviously was very touched by the gift. I used to see her wear the coat I gave her with great pride.

SHARING MY HOME TO HELP

In another situation, my wife and I allowed a single mother and her two children to live in our home about three months. During their stay, I went away on a business trip and I decided to surprise the kids by buying toys for them. They were both pre-teens. One child met me at the door and his brother was in another room. The child who met me at the door received the gift and started running around and around in circles and yelling to his brother. He repeatedly yelled to his brother as he ran in circles saying, "We have gifts!" He went on and on until he finally opened the gifts. The children were very thankful and very excited. Their faces were all aglow and I was about as happy as they were. It was almost like Christmas morning!

SPECIAL GIFT TO MY SICK AUNT

When I lived in Texas, one of my aunts became very ill and I decided to go by her home to visit her. She lived in Austin, TX. During the visit, I gave her several gifts. The gifts were not expensive but I just wanted to bring comfort and cheer to my aunt because I knew that she was a wonderful person and was quite ill. She was a warm, friendly, kind, gentle, soft-spoken person.

She would sweep me off my feet with her love, warmth and beautiful, slow, melodic speech. Not only did she have a beautiful personality but her face was beautiful also. My wife and I would just love to go to her home. Regardless of whatever time of day it was, when you went to her home, she would always offer to prepare a meal for you. Sometimes we would accept her offer and I would sit down at that table and make that food vanish. I would enjoy every bite of those wonderful meals.

Because of the beautiful person she was, I wanted to express my love and appreciation by providing her with several small gifts. Given that she was quite ill, I knew I might not ever see her again. One of the gifts that I bought her was a stuffed animal (a teddy bear). I didn't really know how much the gifts would mean to her but I was later told that each night before she went to bed she would say, "Where is that teddy bear that Calvin bought me?

I want to put it in the bed so I can sleep with it." When I heard this I was surprised and overjoyed. I was so happy to know that! I never saw her again because she lived many miles from me and my schedule was always so busy.

I cherish the fact that the last time I saw her I took a gift that she deemed to be very special. She went on to be with the Lord and I was able to speak at her home going service. If you love someone, then you should express your love through giving. God set the example as He gave His only begotten Son to save the world. We too should give and bless other people.

GIVE AND IT SHALL BE GIVEN

Luke 6:38 (CEV)
*"If you **give** to others, you will be given a **full amount in return.** It will be packed down, shaken together and spilling over into your lap. The way you treat others is the way you will be treated."*

When I was about to step behind the pulpit in church, a man came to me and told me that he had been greatly blessed because people had given him car after car. He was an auto mechanic and people often gave him cars. I asked him, "What are you doing with all those cars?" He responded, "Right now I'm just keeping them." Then I said, "You have so many cars that you need to start giving some of those cars away. If you do, God will bless you."

He apparently could see the wisdom in what I told him. He acted very quickly and he gave a car to a person who was a single parent. Because he acted so quickly and willingly, I felt led to take up a collection for him. I told the people in the church to give any sum of money they desired to the generous auto mechanic. I said those who gave would quickly get blessings as a result of giving to this man.

GIVE AND RECEIVE

People started blessing the man with gift after gift. The money continually came in. When they finished, the man had a sizable sum of money. The man was so happy that he had given away that car. One of the givers was a Pastor who happened to be visiting from another state. A few days after the mechanic received the gifts, I heard from the Pastor who had visited my church. The Pastor said that because he gave to the auto mechanic, the following Sunday, his church received the largest offering the church had ever gotten!

The Pastor also said that he felt that the reason his church got the financial blessing was because he had given so freely to the mechanic. He went on to explain that another big gift was made to the church. The second gift was large but was not nearly as large as the prior gift. The Pastor was very grateful, as the money was a great benefit to his church. That Pastor planted a seed and God met the need!

SAVED FROM DESPERATE SITUATION

My wife joined me during a business trip and we selected a hotel where I usually stay when in that city. While I was away at work, the housekeeping department sent someone to our room to clean it.

The lady and my wife struck up a conversation and she told my wife she was going through a number of different problems. She explained to my wife that one of her problems was that she did not have enough money to pay her electric bill. After learning about this problem, my wife prayed for the woman to get help. The next time I saw her, she was in a very pleasant mood. She told me that the prayer that my wife prayed had been quickly answered. Somehow God had met her need and the electric bill had been paid.

About eight or nine weeks later, I went on another business trip to the same city. I returned to the same hotel where my wife and I had stayed. I saw the same woman who had been blessed by the prayer of my wife.

NOWHERE TO TURN

This time, when I saw her, she was in tears. I said to her, "What's the matter?" With tears falling from her eyes she said, "They're going to take my children." I suppose her electricity had been turned off so many times that the relevant state agency officials felt that she was not a responsible parent. I couldn't clearly understand everything she was saying but the outcome was that the state officials had seen enough. As a result, they wanted to take the children out of her custody. I was on the way to breakfast when I saw the woman and I told her to just give me time to eat breakfast and I would pray for her. I told her not to worry because God was going to make sure that everything would be all right.

After I ate breakfast, it was just about time for the woman to clean my room. She came into my room and I made sure that the door was left about half open. I began to pray for her and I asked God to show her some very fast signs that He was on her side. I asked God to let her see almost immediate results because of the prayer.

IMMEDIATE RESPONSE

About thirty-seconds after   I asked God to move quickly to help this woman, there was a knock on the door. Remember, the door was about half open. All the knocking on the door interrupted the prayer. She was very close to the door so she simply opened the door a little wider to see who was there. She found out that a person whose room she had just cleaned wanted to give her an unusually big tip. Realizing what had happened, I explained that the Lord had moved fast to answer the prayer. The woman started shaking, trembling and crying. Then I asked, "When was the last time you got a tip that big?

She told me that it had been a very long time. After the woman received the big tip, I continued to pray and ask that God do whatever was needed to prevent her from losing custody of her children. The next day I asked the other hotel employees where the woman was and they explained she was off that day.

She returned to work a few days later and when I saw her, she had a huge smile. I asked her, "God solved your problem didn't He?" With a big smile on her face she said, "Yes!" She said that on her day off she had gotten a second job and that her new boss immediately paid every penny of the electric bill. She said the second job would not interfere with the old job and that the new job would bless her with enough money to continually keep her electric bill paid and current. As a result the state government would allow her to keep her children. It might sound cliché but God is truly good!

MOVED TO GIVE BACK

The woman was so touched and affected that she wanted to do something in return. Every time I would stay at that hotel, the woman would ask about my wife. She was so grateful that God had used me, as well as my wife, to successfully pray for her situation. She asked me, "Would you please stay in this hotel every time you come to this town?" She said, "Please, please come stay in this hotel. Please, please stay in the section of the hotel that they've assigned to me to clean."

She kept saying, "Please, don't stay at any other hotel but this one." I smiled and said, "Okay." That really touched my heart. Then she said that because she worked at the hotel, one of the perks or fringe benefits of the job was that the hotel gave her a number of free nights at any of the hotels in that particular chain. She said the hotel would allow her to give away a free night to any person of her choosing.

She wanted to give me one of her free nights. She didn't have much to give but she wanted my wife and I to enjoy one of her free nights at any one of the hotels in the chain. I was not led to accept her offer but I didn't want to be impolite. I just said, "Thank you" and I moved on.

WANTED!
"More to improve and fewer to disapprove.
More doers and fewer talkers.
More to say it can be done
and fewer to say it's impossible.
More to inspire others
and fewer to throw cold water on them.
More to get into the thick of things
and fewer to sit on the sidelines.
More to point out what's right
and fewer to show what's wrong.
More to light a candle
and fewer to curse the darkness."
- Unknown

9

SUCCESS THROUGH PRAYER

Hebrews 11:6 (CEV)
*"But without faith no one can please God. We must believe that God is real and that **he rewards everyone who searches for him**."*

Did you know that there are about 650 different prayers in the Bible? From Genesis to Revelation, the Bible has many, many examples of how to pray. There are those prayers that God honors and those that God does not honor. I want to make sure I'm praying the prayers God *will* answer, don't you?

~~~~~~~~~~~~~~~~~~~~

Prayer is one of the most vital subjects in the Word of God.

~~~~~~~~~~

Let's start out by looking at how the Bible defines prayer. Here are six references that I love. They reveal how the Bible defines prayer:

A lifting up our soul to God: Psalm 25:1 (ESV) "To you, O Lord, I lift up my soul"; Psalm 143:8 (ESV) "Let me hear in the morning of your steadfast love, for in you I trust. Make me know the way I should go, for to you I lift up my soul."

A pouring out our heart to God: Psalm 62:8 (CEV) "Trust God, my friends and always tell him each one of your concerns. God is our place of safety."

A crying out to God: Psalm 86:3 (KJV) "Be merciful unto me, O Lord: for I cry unto thee daily"; Psalm 84:2 (KJV) "My soul longeth, yea, even fainteth for the courts of the Lord: my heart and my flesh crieth out for the living God."

Coming before the throne of grace: Hebrews 4:16 (AMP) "Let us then fearlessly and confidently and boldly draw near to the throne of grace (the throne of God's unmerited favor to us sinners), that we may receive mercy [for our failures] and find grace to help in good time for every need [appropriate help and well-timed help, coming just when we need it]."

Spiritual sacrifice & the fruit of our lips: Hebrews 13:15 (CEV) "Our sacrifice is to keep offering praise to God in the name of Jesus."

Drawing close to God in friendship, fellowship and trust: James 4:8 (GW) "Come close to God and he will come close to you. Clean up your lives, you sinners and clear your minds, you doubters."

SUPPLICATION

The prayers that I'm going to discuss here are mostly prayers of supplication. Prayers of supplication are petitions for a personal request (Philippians 4:6) "Be careful for nothing; but in every thing by prayer and supplication with thanksgiving let your requests be made known unto God." There are several *types of prayers of supplication* too, such as:

Wisdom: James 1:5-8 (KJV) "If any of you lack wisdom, let him ask of God, that giveth to all men liberally and upbraideth not; and it shall be given him. But let him ask in faith, nothing wavering. For he that wavereth is like a wave of the sea driven with the wind and tossed. For let not that man think that he shall receive any thing of the Lord. A double minded man is unstable in all his ways."

Daily needs: Mathew 6:33 (NIV) "But seek first his kingdom and his righteousness and all these things will be given to you as well."

Resisting temptation: Matthew 26:41 (ESV) "Watch and pray that you may not enter into temptation. The spirit indeed is willing but the flesh is weak."

Intercessions for others: James 5:16 (NLT) "Confess your sins to each other and pray for each other so that you may be healed. The earnest prayer of a righteous person has great power and produces wonderful results." Acts 8:24; Ex 32:11; Genesis 18:23-33. Everyone who claims to be a child of God should be drawing close to God in friendship, fellowship and trust:

James 4:8 (CEV)
*"**Come near to God and he will come near to you.** Clean up*
your lives, you sinners. Purify your hearts, you people who can't
make up your mind."

When I became aware of the promises and blessings of God, I started diligently seeking Him. For years and years I have spent intense and quality time in prayer, fasting, reading and studying God's Word. As a result, God started answering my prayers. As I stated before, I have long desired to help people in need.

PRAY AS GOD DESIRES

Even though God wants to answer our prayers, He has told us in His Word what we must do to get our prayers answered. First, He wants us to pray fervently to get effective results. We should pray like we mean it and show excitement, enthusiasm, zeal and intensity. We must pray strong, sincere, touching, heartfelt prayers.

We should not pray weak, halfhearted, nonchalant prayers like someone speaking in a library. As we well know people who speak in the library speak softly to keep from disturbing others. As distinguished from library speech, our prayers should be heartfelt, strong and encouraging. This is why there are so many places in the Bible where we see "cry out to the Lord" (Joel 1:14), "cry out day and night" (Luke 18:7) and "he cried out to God all night" (1 Samuel 15:11).

BELIEVING IS IMPERATIVE

Furthermore, God wants us to believe that He is going to answer our prayers. He wants us to believe the promises He has made to us in the Bible. The scripture tells us that, "If thou canst believe, all things are possible to him that believeth" (Mark 9:23).

The Word of God also says that whatever we ask in prayer, we will receive it, if we believe (Mark 11:24). We are supposed to have faith in the words and promises of God. How do we get faith? According to Romans 10:17, faith (or the belief in the words and promises of God) comes as a result of hearing the words and promises of God. By hearing the positive and powerful words of the Bible, faith will come and be deposited in our hearts. The glorious and life changing Word of God *must* be heard many, many times for us to get the necessary amount of faith that God wants us to get!

If we believe God's promises strongly enough, then God will move to *help* us and give us what *we* desire. The Bible also says that, "with God all things are possible" (Matthew 19:26). Moreover, the Bible tells us that when we pray, we *must* pray in the name of Jesus. Let's look at the words Jesus spoke regarding prayer. In the book of John Jesus says,

John 14:13-14 (ESV)

*"Whatever you ask **in my name**, this I will do, that the Father may be glorified in the Son. 14 If you ask me anything in my name, I will do it."*

John 16:23 (CEV)

*"When that time comes, you won't have to ask me about anything. I tell you for certain that the Father will give you whatever you ask for **in my name**."*

We must make our prayer requests to God in the name of Jesus because **the name of Jesus is above every name** according to Philippians 2:9. When we pray in the name of Jesus, we are asking God to respect and honor the prayer the same way He would if Jesus had spoken the prayer.

GOD KNOWS YOUR NEEDS

I had lunch with a man who had an old smoking car. I felt badly for the man. Immediately after lunch, I started praying very hard for him. I could sense that God was going to do a great work in his life.

A few days later the man got a large sum of money and he used it to get a new car. Overjoyed, he was at a loss of words to try to tell me what God had done for him. He was able to specifically connect my prayer to the receipt of a large sum of money that enabled him to get the new car that he badly needed.

God really does want us to succeed in life. *He wants you to have your needs met!* The Bible says in Philippians 4:19 (KJV), "But my God shall supply all your need, according to His riches in glory by Christ Jesus."

PRAYER BRINGS MIRACLES

I have prayed for people that were being evicted and getting foreclosed on, they needed to get homes and they got homes. I have prayed for people to get jobs and the jobs came. I have prayed for people to get job promotions and the Lord blessed them to get the promotions.

I have even prayed for athletes to succeed and excel and the Lord answered and showed them great and unusual favor. I have prayed for people to get healed of various sicknesses and diseases and God has healed them. Truly our God supplies all our need and prayer is the most widely used method to get God to help us. It is great to see people's lives turn around after the Lord gives them help.

PRAYER SAVES A MEDICAL CAREER

Hebrews 4:16 (ESV)
"Let us then with confidence draw near to the throne of grace, that we may receive mercy and find grace to help in time of need."

I once met a medical doctor who felt that he had been unjustly deprived of the right to practice medicine **only** because of his complexion and national origin. He explained that he was a doctor who delivered babies (an obstetrician/gynecologist-OBGYN) but was deprived of that opportunity due to discrimination. The doctor stated that to earn a living in this medical specialty, he had to deliver many babies. He told me that he had to have hospital "privileges" at any hospital where he wanted to send his patients to have their babies delivered.

He further explained that the word "privileges" refers to permission from the proper hospital authorities to come into a hospital to treat patients. The doctor also pointed out that without being able to go into the hospital to treat patients or deliver babies; his pay and fees would be so low that he couldn't earn a decent living. He said he followed all the rules and properly delivered babies but the people who ran the hospital didn't like him because of his complexion and national origin.

As a result, he said that they took his "privileges" away. He said that for two years he had tried to get another job but the hospital would always give him a bad reference. He said that, for these reasons he couldn't really earn a living in that town or any other town.

FOCUS ON THE POSITIVE

Remember, I said always focus on the positive and not the negative. If you are a racecar driver, you should never focus on the wall that you want to avoid. If you are a football player, you will never say to a teammate, "man don't drop that ball," especially if it's a close game! The players have to focus on holding the ball and not focus on the possibility of dropping the ball. In the case of the doctor, whose career I was trying to save, I didn't focus on discrimination or racial prejudice. Instead, I focused on getting the doctor a new job.

I lifted up an "effectual fervent prayer" to God to get the man a new job. *In 24 hours*...the man got a new job after he had tried, unsuccessfully, for two long years to get one. The doctor was delighted, overjoyed and super excited. His career was saved through an "effectual fervent prayer."

DEBT ELIMINATED THROUGH PRAYER

On a number of occasions I have prayed for people who had overwhelming debts or financial problems and God removed these burdens. Let me give you an example. A woman came to me in church one day and explained that she had incurred a debt that proved to be a big burden on her. She had become aware that I had experienced success in praying for people who had big problems, including money problems.

She had limited resources and was having a very hard time trying to pay this debt. This was a number of years ago and I believe she owed around $4,000, not to mention all the other bills she had to pay. She was stressed out and she didn't know how to solve her financial problems. I prayed very hard for this woman and believed that God would help her with this debt. The very next week she came to me after church and told me that she had gotten in touch with the creditor. She said the creditor told her that there were *no records* showing that she owed them! She gave a great testimony and expressed great joy that the burdensome debt had been removed.

RENT PROBLEM SOLVED

I have been able to go before God to get help for a number of other people who were going through financial hardships and troubles. The Lord moved greatly and mightily to solve the financial problems of these people. For instance, a friend of mine, who was in a dire financial jam, called me asking for prayer. He was in danger of being evicted from his apartment.

I prayed and went before God to get this problem solved. After I prayed, my friend decided to talk to the landlord about the trouble he was having concerning paying the rent. The landlord told my friend that the rental office records showed that the *rent had been paid*! Somehow, the rent problem vanished. Talk about happy! My friend acted like a child who had just gotten gifts at Christmas. While I couldn't be as happy as my friend, I was overjoyed.

PRAYER CHANGES MISGUIDED WOMAN

You may have heard the often-used expression, "Prayer changes things," and "God is good." The phrase "God is good" is popular and very widely used. Many people may not know it but there are scriptures that in essence say, "God is good." One such scripture says, "Oh give thanks to the Lord, for He is good" (1 Chronicle 16:34).

Another scripture says that whatever we ask for in prayer we will receive what we request if we believe (Mark 11:24). The Bible says we should always pray. As we journey through life we meet, come across and face many types of conditions and people. When I was a single man years ago, I worked in a relatively large federal office building. One day when I was at work, I went out to a restaurant for lunch. After I finished eating, I rushed back to the job because I had a great deal of work to do. I had to review many papers such as legal briefs and court complaints. Because I supervised attorneys, I had many management duties and I always had deadlines to meet.

RESIST TEMPTATION

As I was rushing to get on the elevator, an attractive woman spoke to me and said something like, "Hey handsome you sure are looking good in that suit." Then she said, "What's your name?" I told her my name and then she said something like, "What's your number?" At that point I looked at the ring finger of her left hand and I said, "Aren't you married?" She said, "Yes" and then I said, *"You like to live dangerously and I don't."* At that point, I quickly walked away and got on the elevator. When I returned to the office, I was moved to quickly pray for the married woman who had just made an improper pass at me. I asked God to open this person's eyes to show her that she was headed down the wrong road. Furthermore, I asked the Lord to show her that she needed to change her ways and live a life that was pleasing to God.

About an hour after I prayed, someone brought a note to me from the woman who had just flirted with me. The note read: "Dear Mr. Washington, I sincerely apologize to you for talking to you the way I did. I am a church going woman and I don't know what came over me. I don't act like I did with you. Please forgive me for what I did." The woman had been touched by God to change her ways. The prayer worked to bring the woman to her senses and I was glad to be a vessel used by God to influence her to change her ways.

MY WIFE THE GREAT PRAYER WARRIOR

Prayer is our basic spiritual weapon and we should use it often and liberally if we want to lead successful and victorious lives. A number of years ago I took my wife, Nicole, to look at a house. Inside the house I walked through a number of rooms and then went to the bathroom. My wife remained in the living room. Then all of a sudden, I heard loud voices coming from the living room. After I had gone to the bathroom, a woman who was drunk showed up. She started talking loudly and belligerently, freely spewing profanity and vulgarities (she was *very* drunk).

My wife remained calm, as the woman got increasingly aggressive. Spittle was coming from her mouth, almost landing on my wife. The woman continued to use foul language and refused to leave. When I heard all the loud noise and commotion, I returned to the living room to see what was going on. I heard Nicole tell the woman to leave and stop causing trouble.

"Tomorrow belongs to the people who prepare for it today."
-African Proverb

PRAY WITH FORCE

Then, I heard my wife praying loudly with *force* and *fervor*. Then the drunken woman said, "What you 'pose to be, some kind of *Holy Roller?*" Nicole didn't answer but she just kept right on praying. A few seconds after that, I saw something that I had never seen in my whole entire life. Before I could really figure out what was taking place, the drunken woman got a strange look on her face as my wife continued to pray. *The more my wife prayed the more the drunken woman started to get quiet.* I was still puzzled. But I was able to see that my wife was in control and I started praying. Then all of a sudden, instead of being aggressive, the woman quickly made a move.

She didn't move toward my wife but instead, she moved backward, then my wife moved forward. After moving backward, the woman spun completely around and hurriedly made a mad dash toward the front door. She acted as if a police officer had yelled at her and told her to leave the house or she would be arrested. I assure you, no police officer was present. She simply rushed out to her car, got in it, backed it up and sped off!

THE POWER OF GOD HITS

As I watched the woman get quiet, spin around and head for the front door, it looked so unusual. It seemed like I was in a dream. Inside, I thought, "Is this for real?" I felt like I was watching a Christian movie in which the star of the show was used by God to get out of a jam.

No one tried to hit the woman, hold her or harm her in any way. Evidently, the prayer had been so powerful that the drunken woman simply couldn't stand to hear it. I believe that's why she quickly went to the front door, got in her car and sped away as if someone had pulled a gun or knife on her. Nicole didn't use a physical weapon but she used the spiritual weapon of effectual fervent prayer. "The effectual fervent prayer of a righteous man availeth much (James 5:16)." My wife was protected by the power of prayer and the favor of God. I have no doubt that my wife's prayer prevented a potentially violent incident from taking place on that day!

The scripture says that the Lord is a very present help in times of trouble. "God is our refuge and strength, a very present help in trouble" (Psalm 46:1). He wants to come to our aid when we pray. The precondition of getting God to help us is that we must believe God's Word and that He wants to help us. I get great pleasure when I am able to come to the aid of others.

I obviously can't do everything God does but I can help others through prayer, giving, teaching, counseling and divinely inspired guidance to become more successful in life. So can you! That's why I'm taking so much time and space to give you real-life, today examples of the power of God that works through a yielded vessel.

MAN HEALED OF CANCER

I was asked one time to pray for a man who was stricken with prostate cancer. He had been a very robust person before my meeting him but still had a strong and commanding voice. He had suffered off and on with several illnesses but cancer had become the priority.

On his request, I went to his home with a member of my church to pray for him. He was scheduled for surgery in five days. Before I began to pray, I laid hands on the man. I began to pray and use many of the spiritual weapons that God has revealed in His Word. For about three hours, I "fought the good fight of faith." The man was so overjoyed; he thanked and praised God so deeply, it almost brought us to tears. As always, when I pray for people with dire sicknesses, I asked him to try to get more tests and x-rays before surgery. Instead, he went ahead with the surgery. He was cut open but the surgeon could *not find any cancer*. So, he was stitched back up, held for recovery and released to go home!

The best part of the praise report was he remained cancer free for many, many years. Additionally, God freed him from the addiction to alcohol. He never touched a drop of alcohol again. He has since gone to be with the Lord now but he remained free of prostate cancer and alcoholism until his last day on earth!

WOMAN HEALED OF CANCER

A good woman that I have personally known all my life was diagnosed with cancer of the kidney. She came to me for prayer before her scheduled surgery date. She was scheduled to have surgery three or four weeks after I met with her for prayer. Again, I began to pray and use many of the spiritual weapons that God has revealed in His Word. She was scheduled to have her cancerous kidney removed. Once the surgeons had her opened up and were going to remove her kidney, they could find *no cancer*! As far as I know, she remains cancer free to this day.

WOMAN WITH BLEEDING PROBLEM

Mark 5:25-26 (CEV)
*"In the crowd was a woman who had **been bleeding for twelve** **years**. [26] She had gone to many doctors and they had not done anything except cause her a lot of pain. She had paid them all the money she had. But **instead of getting better, she only got** **worse**."*

She felt that if she could only get to Jesus and touch His clothing, she would be healed. When she saw Jesus, she came behind Him and touched his clothing. Jesus sensed that power had gone out of His body to bring healing to the woman. After the woman touched the clothing of Jesus, she was healed.

PRESENT DAY ISSUE OF BLOOD

I had never thought about a woman in our contemporary world experiencing a continual flow of blood. Of all the physical challenges that women have had that I have prayed for, nobody *ever* faced this. A few years ago a young woman came to me and explained that, just like the woman in the Bible, she too had been bothered by a continual flow of blood.

This problem lasted for *over two years*. She said she was weak, fatigued, depressed and of course, stressed out. She was young, vibrant, single and in the prime of her life. She was very concerned that the excessive bleeding was going to cause her to go into early menopause. She was aware that going into menopause too soon might make her infertile and prevent her from being able to have children. Her greatest desire was to have *five* kids! That was a miracle in itself, because for years, she said she did not want kids at all.

At that point in my life, I *knew* that with God *all* things *are* possible. I diligently prayed with her for the continual bleeding to completely stop. Guess what happened…the bleeding STOPPED!

Several months later, she had *no cycle at all*. This went on for about two more years! She simply had no cycle. Aware that this was also a major problem, she came back to me for more prayer. I prayed with her for a considerable time. I did not pray for her cycle to simply start, instead, I prayed for her body to become regular and a *normal* cycle to manifest.

The next time I saw her, she told me her cycle was normal. Recently, with a glow on her face, she told me she has been *healed for well over five years!* She gives thanks, praise and glory to God for doing a great and wonderful work in her life. She now believes that when she gets married, she will be able to successfully have kids and reap one of God's great blessings. She feels that this major healing is one of the *most important* events that's ever taken place in her life!

IMPORTANT POINT

Matthew 6:5-6 (NIV)
"And when you pray, do not be like the hypocrites, for they love to pray standing in the synagogues and on the street corners to be seen by others. Truly I tell you, they have received their reward in full. ⁶ But when you pray, go into your room, close the door and pray to your Father, who is unseen. Then your Father, who sees what is done in secret, will reward you."

I could share many other stories about people who have been healed, blessed, delivered and set free through this ministry. People with cancer and tumors have been healed on a great number of occasions. In the same way that God has used me to successfully pray for people, He desires to do that through you too! I will discuss this more deeply in *another* book.

~~~~~~~~~~~~~~~~~~~~
Prayer must become as easy and effortless to us as the beating of our hearts.
~~~~~~~~~~~

10

MATURING IN THE CALL

"Without continual growth and progress, such words as improvement, achievement and success have no meaning."
-Benjamin Franklin

Unfortunately, there are people who don't think it takes much time or effort to live a life of good success in the kingdom of God. Many have the attitude that if they get saved today, all the blessings of God should just plop in their laps on tomorrow. Sorry but that's not how the kingdom works.

WHAT PRICE WILL YOU PAY?

"I have been impressed with the urgency of doing. Knowing is not enough; we must apply. Being willing is not enough; we must do."
–Leonardo da Vinci

Everything in life comes with a price. I did not just walk out of the cotton field and walk into Howard University School of Law. I did not just accept Jesus one day and go out and lay hands on people to be healed from cancer the next. Thank God, I did eventually get into Howard Law and God has used me to get many people healed from cancer and other diseases but *it did not happen overnight.*

Your attitude (we discussed attitude in chapter 4) can't be just...read a book (even if it's this one), see a counselor, attend a conference or two, make a fresh commitment to God, shed a few tears at an altar, memorize a few verses . . . and presto, I'm a mature, godly Believer. *If only it were that easy!* Here are some steps that you can take, that will help the process, *if* you adhere to them and don't stumble and fumble around like I did for so many years.

TAKE RESPONSIBILITY

Don't blame others for the failures and troubles in your life. That's too easy and it is unfair. If you were to take a good look at most of the problems you face, you'd probably see that *you* caused them. *Avoid engaging in the blame game.* Don't make excuses for yourself. Take charge of your life and do what is right for you and others.

FIND OUT WHAT MOTIVATES YOU

What excites you enough to do what you have never done before to change your life? Many people are motivated by love, self-preservation, anger (revenge through success), financial gain, rejection and fear. Whatever you find your passion and motivation to be, it's going to require:

enthusiasm, a positive outlook, a positive attitude and a belief in the gifts God has given you and your God-given potential to excel.

STOP PROCRASTINATING

If you're a constant procrastinator, you know the trouble that comes with putting things off. When we procrastinate, we squander away our free time and put off important tasks we should be doing, until it's too late to do them. David says in Psalm 119:60, "I made haste and delayed not to keep thy commandments." That's my advice for you today. Make haste for the things of God. Don't put God off. Don't be too busy for God! Don't put off until tomorrow, what you *should* do today.

"You may delay but time will not."
-Benjamin Franklin

HOW YOU THINK IS EVERYTHING

Always be positive. Think *Success*, not *Failure*. Beware of a negative environment. Without the right attitude it is nearly impossible to please God. Someone once said, "Your attitude is like a flat tire. Until you fix it you are not going anywhere." Be determined to have a good attitude about your life whatever your circumstances are. Know that for every problem, God has a solution!

YOUR BELIEF THAT GOD WILL DO ALL THINGS MUST BE UNWAVERING

I can do all things through Christ, who gives me strength (see Philippians 4:13). The moment you say to yourself "I can't," *you won't*. My parents always told me to *never say* I can't. A Pastor friend of mine once said, "It is ok to visit pity city but you can't stay and there comes a time when you need to leave." Positive things happen to positive people.

WRITE DOWN YOUR DREAMS & TAKE ACTION

Make yourself a list or a vision board. In Habakkuk 2:2, God says, "...Write the vision and make it plain upon tables, that he may run that readeth it." For this book, I had to take action and start writing. Everyday I try to do something to help my family and myself progress forward in life. You've got to start *somewhere* and do *something*. Even if you take baby steps, you're closer than you were before those steps were taken!

KEEP YOUR FOCUS

There are so many distractions in life. Don't let other people or things distract you.

Matthew 14:29-30 (GW)
*"Jesus said, "Come!" So Peter got out of the boat and walked on the water toward Jesus. But **when he noticed how strong the wind was, he became afraid and started to sink**. He shouted, "Lord, save me!"*

Some people will deliberately get you off focus to ensure you fail at whatever it is you are trying to do. Watch out for them. They will be wolves in sheep's clothing. Instead, surround yourself with positive people that believe in you. Don't be distracted by the naysayers or prognosticators of doom and gloom.

DON'T LET FEAR STOP YOU

2 Timothy 1:7 (ESV)
*"For God gave us a spirit **not of fear** but of power and love and self-control."*

"Feed your faith and your fears will starve to death."
-Unknown

The forces of evil to hinder, cripple, discourage and defeat people often use fear. It sometimes paralyzes people and stops them from moving forward to achieve their goals and dreams.

If you believe in God, all things are possible, including the defeat and elimination of fear. The scripture says in:

Psalm 27:1 (CEV)
*"You, Lord, are the light that keeps me safe. I am not afraid of anyone. You protect me and **I have no fears.**"*

BE AWARE OF YOUR THOUGHTS

**"As a single footstep will not make a path on the earth,
so a single thought will not make a pathway in the mind. To make
a deep physical path, we walk again and again. To make a deep
mental path, we must think over and over the kind
of thoughts we wish to dominate our lives."
-Henry David Thoreau**

Your thoughts—those little voices you listen to all day long in your head—act like a seed in that they get planted (program your brain) and grow (affect your behavior). Take a closer look at what you are thinking to yourself. The Bible tells us to be transformed by the renewing of your mind (Romans 12:2) and to take every thought captive to the obedience of Christ (2 Corinthians 10:5). We *must* purpose to think good wholesome and positive thoughts. Are you thinking good things about yourself or are you thinking bad things about yourself?

THE POWER OF WORDS

Interestingly, God used words to frame the world (Hebrews 11:3). We are not God but we can use words to produce either positive or negative conditions. We were created in the image of God and He told us to be fruitful and multiply and to subdue the earth and to exercise dominion over animals and creatures on earth (Genesis 1:27-28).

Ephesians 4:29 (CEV)
*"Stop all your dirty talk. **Say the right thing at the right time**
and help others by what you say."*

We should follow the instructions of God. We should not play the blame game or speak negatively of others. Lean on Jesus and move on in life. The Word of God admonishes us to,

Ephesians 4:31-32 (ESV)
***"Let all bitterness and wrath and anger and clamor and slander be put away from you**, along with all malice. ³² Be kind to one another, tenderhearted, forgiving one another, as God in Christ forgave you."*

Be careful what you let come out of your mouth! Once you say something, good or bad, it is released to the universe and it *cannot be taken back*. Your words can be used to produce life or death, victory or defeat. Mark 11:23 says, that if you believe the words that you speak, you will get what you say. Watch your words.

PASSION

Passion is to attitude, as breathing is to life. Passion enables you to apply your gifts more effectively. It's the burning desire that communicates commitment, determination and spirit. People can hear it in your voice. It's infectious. The great abolitionist Harriet Tubman once said, "Every great dream begins with a dreamer. Always remember, you have within you the strength, the patience and the passion to reach for the stars to change the world."

Through her bravery, courage, strength and passion, she led many slaves to freedom. She realized that one of the preconditions of her success was to have great passion to lead her people to freedom. Passion is a powerful emotion that serves to push you forward, make you stay focused and moves you to succeed and excel. Passion helps you to produce results.

LIGHTEN UP

Proverbs 17:22 (ESV)
"A joyful heart is good medicine but a crushed spirit dries up the bones."

Job 8:21 (ESV)
"He will yet fill your mouth with laughter and your lips with shouting."

Joy displays strength and peace. It causes you to focus on the positive and not on the negative. The Bible says, "The joy of the Lord is your strength" (Nehemiah 8:10). The more laughter in your life, the less stress you'll have, which means more positive energy to help you put your *good success* plan, into action! My wife and I love to laugh. On family nights, sometimes we laugh so hard, we all start crying and until our sides are hurting.

BE PERSISTENT AND NEVER GIVE UP

Paul tells Timothy in 2 Timothy 4:7 (NIV), "I have fought the good fight, I have finished the race, I have kept the faith." Success in Christ Jesus is a marathon, not a sprint. Never give up!

"Nothing in this world can take the place of persistence. Talent will not: nothing is more common than unsuccessful men with talent. Genius will not; unrewarded genius is almost a proverb. Education will not: the world is full of educated derelicts. Persistence and determination alone are omnipotent."
-Calvin Coolidge

Every story of good success I have ever read entails long hard hours of dedication. There is no getting around this.

Luke 11:9 (ESV)
"And I tell you, ask and it will be given to you; seek and you will find; knock and it will be opened to you."

2 Thessalonians 3:13 (ESV)
"As for you, brothers, do not grow weary in doing good."

1 Thessalonians 5:17 (ESV)
"pray without ceasing,"

SLEEP AND FATIGUE PROBLEMS

When I was a child, I started having trouble with sleepiness and fatigue and it seemed that I was always sleepy when no one else was. People would laugh at me and call me "sleepy head." This problem would bother me so much that I would almost cry. I was never able to watch television at night or do many of the things my friends did at night.

As I grew older the problem seemed to get worse. Throughout high school, college and even law school, I had trouble staying awake. I didn't get discouraged because I felt *compelled* to continue to move forward to get an education. In college and law school I would drink so much coffee to stay awake, I got tired of seeing coffee. I got tired of drinking and even smelling coffee.

THE LAW IS A JEALOUS MISTRESS

Once I entered law school, I soon learned that the study of law was very time consuming and demanding. I studied many hours both day and night. Justice Joseph Story, a United States Supreme Court Justice in the nineteenth century gave a very good description of the study of law. He pointed out that, "The law is a jealous mistress and requires a long and constant courtship. It's not won by trifling favors."

I quickly learned that Justice Story was most correct. Law School was like a jealous lover who wanted every minute of my time. I had to study on weekends, early in the morning, late at night and even on holidays. The long hours of study were made even more difficult by the trouble I had staying awake. Fatigue and sleepiness seemed to torment me. I would usually fall asleep with the law books wide open. Sometimes I would be so sleepy I would accidentally drop the law books on the floor when I fell asleep.

Out of frustration, I came up with the idea that it might help me to stay awake if I would put on my swimming trunks, get in a tub of hot water and do my studying there. To my amazement this practice worked! I would run a tub of *hot water*, get my law books and study in the hot water for hours and hours. When the water got cold, I would refill the tub with hot water. Sometimes I would stay in the tub for *twelve to fourteen hours at a time*.

DO MORE, GET MORE

Even when I graduated from law school and studied for the bar examination to become an attorney, I would fill the tub with hot water, get in the tub and study for many hours. When I studied for the bar examination, I sometimes got tired of studying in the tub to fight the sleepiness and fatigue. Realizing that I had to do whatever I could to stay awake, I would sometimes leave the apartment. To remain awake and alert I would go to a nearby baseball stadium and use the discomfort of the stadium bleachers to keep myself awake and alert to study for the bar exam. I would be the only person in the stadium! It was scary but I was desperate.

By using the stadium bleachers, I was also able to avoid the distraction of turning on the television or going into the refrigerator for snacks or drinks. Sometimes I would sit on those bleachers of the baseball stadium until the sun went down.

"What we hope ever to do with ease,
we must first learn to do with diligence."
-Samuel Johnson

When it became too dark for me to study in the baseball stadium, I would return to the apartment and go back to studying in the tub. My practice of studying in the bathtub and the baseball stadium served me well. I was able to pass the bar examination in my home state of Texas. Many people *fail* the bar examination the first time they take it. Some people never pass at all. Thank God, I passed the bar exam the first time I took it!

"One of the marks of spiritual maturity is the quiet confidence
that God is in control – without the need to understand
why He does what He does."
-Anonymous

MY FREEDOM COMES

After passing the bar examination, I was able to get a job with the federal government. Once I got the job, the problem with sleepiness and fatigue got worse. Many times I would have trouble staying awake on the job. I simply could not hold my eyes open. There were times when the sleepiness *would* let up and I was able to focus and properly concentrate on my work.

At other times I would have to depend on coffee to keep me alert and awake. In spite of the many periods of sleepiness, I was still able to succeed on my job. I would often get praise and compliments from high-level officials who were impressed with my work. On one occasion I received a cash award for great work and I even got a favorable write up from Clarence Thomas who, as I mentioned before, was the highest-ranking official of the agency where I worked.

After working a number of years as an attorney, I eventually accepted Jesus as my Lord and Savior as I pointed out before. One evening I attended a service at a relatively large church. After the sermon ended, the Pastor told the congregation that those who needed prayer should come to the altar at the front of the church. After suffering with the sleepiness and fatigue problem all of my life, I decided to go to the front of the church for prayer.

The Pastor and other ministers were fervently praying for many people. When the Pastor finally reached me, I told him that I needed prayer for the lifelong problem of unusual sleepiness and fatigue. He listened carefully to what I told him. To my surprise, he just stared at me for a short time.

Then, he started to pray for me. When he finished praying, I returned to my seat wondering if the prayer had changed me in any way. As time passed, I noticed that I no longer had trouble with the sleepiness and fatigue. The prayer worked wonders for me. It has been many years since the Pastor prayed for me and from that time to this day, I have never again had trouble from excessive sleepiness and fatigue.

RESIST TEMPTATION

"Fly from all occasions of temptation and if still tempted, fly further still. If there is no escape possible, then have done with running away and show a bold face and take the two-edged sword of the Spirit. Some temptations must be taken by the throat as David killed the lion; others must be stifled as David hugged the bear to death. Some you had better keep to yourselves and not give air. Shut them up as a scorpion in a bottle. Scorpions in such confinement die soon but if allowed out for a crawl and then put back into the bottle and corked down, they will live a long while and give you trouble. Keep the cork on your temptations, and they will die of themselves."
-Unknown

11

SUCCESS BLOCKERS

"The road to success is always under construction."
-Anonymous

Most people want to succeed and excel in life. We spend our lives trying to obtain happiness, joy, peace, prosperity, recognition, rewards, comfort and achievement. There are many obstacles, barriers, hindrances, road blockers and mountains to keep us from obtaining the success and things we desire in life. Everyone who lives on this planet is going to sooner or later experience problems, difficulties and concerns. Human beings are confronted with sickness, indebtedness, fears, insecurities, setbacks, poverty, conflicts, burdens, infirmities and various other problems.

The challenges of life are not peculiar to just one particular race, sex, color or nationality. Cancer attacks the young and old. Divorce occurs in rich families, poor families and middle-class families. Drug addiction can occur in the life of anyone who chooses to use drugs. Regardless of an individual's physical characteristics or socioeconomic status, *problems are going to arise.*

PROBLEMS ARE EVERYWHERE

Perhaps you have wondered why the various problems of life arise. Some people are even prompted to inquire, "Why me?" They may say, "What have I done to deserve this?" They may conclude that they have not done anything to anyone to deserve the treatment or conditions to which they are exposed.

You may have heard someone make a statement such as, "If God is so good, then why didn't He save my marriage?" You may have heard words such as these: "If God is supposed to protect us, then why did He let Brother Smith die at such a young age?" Such questions deserve an answer. The most important question should be, "how could I overcome the various problems of life?"

THE LAW OF SOWING AND REAPING

From a very broad standpoint and to a large extent, our barriers to success relate to troubles that come on us through the law of sowing and reaping.

Galatians 6:7-9(KJV)

"Be not deceived; God is not mocked: for whatsoever a man soweth, that shall he also reap.⁸ For he that soweth to his flesh shall of the flesh reap corruption; but he that soweth to the Spirit shall of the Spirit reap life everlasting.
⁹ And let us not be weary in well doing: for in due season we shall reap, if we faint not."

Sowing and reaping literally pertain to agriculture. The word sow means to plant. The word "reap" means to gather, accumulate or collect something. It means to harvest something such as a crop. For example, if you plant apple seeds, then you will eventually receive the reward of ripe apples. The time will come when you will be able to gather (reap) the benefit (which is the fruit) of your labor. You will obtain the benefit of your labor when it is time to harvest the apples.

THE LAW OF PROCREATION

It is necessary to understand that everything produces after its kind. This comes from the law of sowing and reaping. This principle (everything produces after its kind), is first mentioned by God in:

Genesis 1:11-12(KJV)
"And God said, Let the earth bring forth grass, the herb yielding seed and the fruit tree yielding fruit after his kind, whose seed is in itself, upon the earth: and it was so.[12] And the earth brought forth grass and herb yielding seed after his kind and the tree yielding fruit, whose seed was in itself, after his kind: and God saw that it was good."

Vegetation produces seeds. Each plant produces a seed. That seed has the capability of producing a plant just like the very plant that the seed came from. The principle we see in operation is that everything produces after its kind. As a result of this principle, apple trees produce apple seeds.

Those apple seeds then produce apple trees. The cycle continues on and on. Everything produces after its kind. In Genesis 1:11-12, the objects (plants) that were produced were good. Why was it good? The Lord says so in verse 11. The Word says, *"and God saw that it was good."*

THE POOL OF BETHESDA

At the pool of Bethesda, Jesus healed a man who had suffered from some type of infirmity for 38 years. The Lord later saw the man in the temple and said to him, "See, you have been made well. Sin no more, lest a worst thing come upon you" (John 5:14).

We can reasonably conclude the man had previously done something sinful to have the infirmity that Jesus healed. He apparently engaged in some type of wrong or misdeed that got him in trouble. So, what does that mean for us?

I believe we too, can end up doing something wrong and end up in a lot of trouble as a result. The lesson we should learn is that *misdeeds, sins and errors can bring trouble, problems and suffering.* Some negative conditions are so burdensome and challenging, they BLOCK SUCCESS! To succeed in life, we must live moral, godly lives to avoid being defeated by the numerous obstacles and barriers brought on by sin and misdeeds.

UNFORGIVENESS

One of the major barriers to a fruitful, productive and successful life is unforgiveness. Once again I must refer to the law of sowing and reaping. What you give out is what you get back in one way or the other. Give love and you will receive love. Give hate and you will receive hate. If you show unforgiveness, then unforgiveness will be shown to you. Family members, friends and those in authority have disappointed us all. Someone may have cheated you out of money, caused you to make a bad investment, paid you unfair wages, denied you a promotion or abused you as a child. This list is by no means exhaustive. I have merely provided a few examples so that you can get the idea.

When you feel that you have been victimized or mistreated, you tend to harbor feelings of bitterness, hatred, animosity and unforgiveness against the person. By holding negative feelings, we set in motion spiritual laws that could have an injurious impact upon our success and well-being.

FORGIVE TO BE FORGIVEN

This is what the Bible says in Mark chapter 11:

Mark 11:25 (NIV)
"And when you stand praying, if you hold anything against anyone,
forgive them, so that your Father in heaven may forgive you
your sins."

This scripture is as plain as day! If you *refuse* to forgive, then God will *refuse* to forgive you. With God holding unforgiveness against you, *how* can you succeed? No one should *ever* want to have this type of status with God. We should take great heed to the instructions of the scripture,

Romans 12:17-21(NLT)
*"**Never pay back evil with more evil**. Do things in such a way that everyone can see you are honorable. [18] Do all that you can to **live in peace with everyone**.[19] Dear friends, never take revenge. Leave that to the righteous anger of God. For the Scriptures say, "I will take revenge; I will pay them back," says the Lord.[20] Instead, "If your enemies are hungry, feed them. If they are thirsty, give them something to drink. In doing this, you will heap burning coals of shame on their heads."[21] **Don't let evil conquer you but conquer evil by doing good**."*

When you show kindness to those who have mistreated you, it will bring peace. It will bring the wrongdoer under conviction to treat you right.

SHOW KINDNESS TO OVERCOME WRONG

"There is only one way to avoid criticism: do nothing, say nothing and be nothing. "
—Aristotle

My wife and I started a church many years ago. We held services in one of the classrooms of a nearby university. There were several start up churches that met across the hall from where we met. Each Sunday, we had to unload and bring in heavy equipment, supplies, musical equipment and everything else needed for a church service.

The place where vehicles parked to unload equipment to carry into the building was narrow and small. One of the churches had a car remaining in the space. They had delayed in moving it and I was busy putting out signs getting ready for service. My wife noticed that the other church was not unloading anymore and had no need to continue to take up the unloading space. They were blocking us from unloading for service. She kindly and politely asked that someone in the other church move his or her vehicle. All we wanted to do was unload our equipment so we could start setting up for service.

BEING THE BIGGER PERSON IS BETTER

The Pastor of the other church somehow got the idea that we were troublemakers who were rude and ungodly. He wrote me a very harsh letter. He felt that he needed to tell us that the members of our church needed to learn how to treat others. I sensed that if I went, "blow for blow" with him, trouble and strife would escalate and get more intense. Being mindful of the Word of God, I decided to forgive. In fact, I wrote the Pastor a nice letter referencing harmony, unity, peace and God's love. I never addressed his insults or accusations.

Most importantly though, I enclosed a large check and said that I wanted God to bless them immensely, with respect to starting their new church. The power of forgiveness and love are amazing. We never again had trouble with that Pastor or his church members. Contradictory to trouble, they would always smile, speak and seem happy and delighted to see us, each time we would pass each other. I believe that because we blessed that church, the Lord moved us from the University classroom to our own freestanding location very quickly after that. We were successful in getting our church a better location.

~~~~~~~~~~~~~~~~~~~~
To be successful in life, we must forgive!
~~~~~~~~~~~

JUDGMENTS

One of the weapons that our adversaries use against us is the spiritual snare called judgments. What is a judgment? I like to define a judgment as an evil opinion, evaluation or attitude in thought or in spoken words that is directed towards someone out of dislike, bitterness, unforgiveness, envy, hatred, jealousy or some other form of evil. The person who does the judging evaluates and assesses the actions of another and condemns that person through bitter thoughts, words or some other type of harmful activity.

JUDGMENTS CAUSE PROBLEMS

When you judge, you activate the law of sowing and reaping. The judgment will trigger negative consequences that will come to pass because the law of sowing and reaping goes into operation from a negative standpoint. Remember, the law can operate to produce either good or evil results.

Why? Everything produces after its kind. Good brings about more good and bad brings about more bad. It is instructive to see what Jesus has to say about judgments:

Matthew 7:1-2 (AMP)
*"**Do not judge and criticize and condemn others**, so that you may not be judged and criticized and condemned yourselves. ² For just as you judge and criticize and condemn others, you will be judged and criticized and condemned and in accordance with the measure you [use to] deal out to others, it will be dealt out again to you."*

What is the Lord saying here? He is telling us that a judgment will trigger the law of sowing and reaping. He is also saying that the type of judgment that is made will cause a similar type of judgment to come back to you. The judgment will produce a *boomerang* effect.

JUDGING AMOUNTS TO CONDEMNATION

In order to fully grasp the meaning of the word "judge" as it is used in Matthew 7:1, let's look at the parallel version of the statements from Luke 6. This is Luke's account of what Jesus said about judging and how good produces more good and evil produces more evil:

Luke 6:37 (KJV)

"Judge not and ye shall not be judged: condemn not and ye shall not be condemned: forgive and ye shall be forgiven"

In making these statements, Jesus is indirectly saying that the law of sowing and reaping is activated by either good or bad behavior. But notice that He uses the word *condemn*. The Lord is saying that we should not engage in judging to the extent that it amounts to condemnation!

What you sow is what you will reap. What goes around comes around. To illustrate, a child who is riding the carousel at an amusement park will go around and then come back around each time the carousel makes a revolution. Judgments operate the same way. Try your best to not judge, so you can avoid being judged yourself. The judgments you make will serve to preclude you from living a victorious, triumphant and successful life in the general area in which the judgment is made. Judgments can serve to *prevent you* from living a successful life.

WORD TRAPS

There are people that don't take the power of what they say seriously. We've discussed this earlier in chapter 5.

Remember Proverbs 18:21? It states that death and life are in the power of the tongue. In Matthew 12:37, Jesus said by our words we'll be justified and by our words we'll be condemned.

The Word reveals that our words can be used to achieve good or evil results. Negative words are word traps; they can produce evil consequences and impede your success. Here are a few examples:

❖I **guess we'll always be poor.** ❖We **will never have anything.** ❖I **just know I'm going to get fired.** ❖If **it wouldn't be for bad luck, I would have no luck at all.** ❖I **was born to lose.** ❖ You **watch, as soon as that car is paid for, it's going to start giving us trouble.** ❖ We **will never be able to pay off all these debts.** ❖Money **just seems to eat a hole in my pocket.** ❖I **will never amount to anything.** ❖I'm **just dumb and stupid.** ❖My **marriage is going to fail.** ❖We're **going to loose everything we've got.** ❖I'm **always sick, all the time.** ❖I'm **always a day late and a dollar short.**

Words like this are released from someone's mouth or consume their thoughts and greatly increase the likelihood that the events spoken of *will come to pass*. Each negative statement serves to contribute to the fulfillment and manifestation of the occurrence that is described.

If you say something is going to occur and you say it long enough, it will eventually come to fruition. I believe that words spoken with force, strong belief and fervor produce the greatest results. Thus, negative words spoken with power and intensity will produce the most powerful negative results.

Similarly, fervent and intense godly words will produce the greatest positive results. I believe these views find support in James 5:16, the effectual fervent prayer of a righteous man avails much. Anything that is done halfheartedly will bring limited results. *Anything that is done with **strong belief, passion** and **intensity** will bring the most noticeable results.*

~~~~~~~~~~~~~~~~~~~~

Research says that we have about 60,000 thoughts a day, as many as 98% of them might be the same as we had the day before and 80% of our thoughts are negative.

Have you ever wondered how many of *your* thoughts God would actually *approve* of?

~~~~~~~~~~

12

GOD'S WILL REGARDING MONEY

"The test of our progress is not whether we add more to the abundance of those who have much; it is whether we provide enough for those who have too little."
— Franklin D. Roosevelt

It does not take a mental giant to understand that money can meet many needs and can be used to achieve many results, both good and evil. Substantial portions of the world's activities revolve around money.

Just think about it, every electronic device that is in existence was manufactured to earn money. Every automobile, every building, every article of furniture and virtually every product of every kind was manufactured or produced to earn money. People sell drugs for money. People sell themselves for money. Most illegal activities are for the sole purpose of making money.

Why does the world engage in all of these activities to make money? The reasons vary from person to person. Looking at this from a broad perspective, people primarily earn money to live comfortably, accomplish their goals, dreams and plans.

They also seek pleasure, happiness, joy, peace, health, success and fame. Furthermore, people acquire money to meet their basic needs, such as food, clothing, shelter, transportation and medical care. Given the wide variety of reasons that people set out to earn money, we as Believers need to discern God's will concerning money. *We need to know the Lord's views on money!*

Money is a substance that for thousands of years, has fascinated, driven and propelled the world. We must determine whether God wants us to be poor, rich or average when it comes to money. If we are to walk in the will of God and be *committed* Believers, we must know how He feels about money.

MISCONCEPTIONS ABOUT MONEY

Many Believers have different views about money and material prosperity. Some people hold the view that Believers are supposed to have only enough money to take care of basic needs. They maintain that Jesus was poor and that His poverty was evidenced by the fact that He was born in a manger.

Additionally, they frequently refer to the scripture that says, the Son of Man has no place even to lay his head. Others point to the Apostles who supposedly were poor, in that Peter remarked, "silver and gold have I none," (Acts 3:6). We are supposed to study the Word of God and rightly divide it, (2

Timothy 2:15). This simply means that we are supposed to study the Bible in the appropriate manner by giving it the proper interpretation and by not taking scriptures out of context.

~~~~~~~~~~~~~~~~~~~

I once heard a man obnoxiously say that he was permitted by scripture to lustfully stare at women because the Bible says, "watch and pray," (Matthew 26:41). Clearly he did not get it right!

~~~~~~~~~~

That misguided man's interpretation of this scripture was totally incorrect. Jesus said that if a man lustfully looks upon a woman, he has committed adultery in his heart (Matthew 5:28). So this man arrived at an erroneous interpretation of the Word through his failure to rightly divide it.

Scripture should be interpreted by referring to other scripture, as well as the setting in which it is written. People often get in trouble by isolating a scripture *they* have determined to be God's will on a particular subject. Similarly, people have interpreted the Bible to mean that God wants us to be poor. I pray that this book will enlighten the eyes of the understanding of every reader!

GOD WANTS US TO PROSPER

3 John 1:2 (KJV)
"Beloved, I wish above all things that thou mayest prosper and be in health, even as thy soul prospereth."

This was a desire by the Apostle John. In fact, the New King James describes John's request as a prayer. In writing this scripture, John would not have made a statement that was inconsistent with the will of God.

~~~~~~~~~~~~~~~~~~~~

Godly financial prosperity is purposed to meet not only your needs and wants but also the needs of others that are less fortunate than you.

~~~~~~~~~~

Clearly, the Word would not contain a desire that ran counter to the will of God, nor would John make a statement that did not line up with the Word of God. Moreover, John wrote this verse under the inspiration of the Holy Spirit. All scripture is inspired by God, as stated in 2 Timothy 3:16. We can conclude from the scripture that God wants us to prosper.

Further proof that God wants us to prosper can be found in 2 Corinthians 8:9:

2 Corinthians 8:9 (AMP)

*"For you are becoming progressively acquainted with and recognizing more strongly and clearly the grace of our Lord Jesus Christ (His kindness, His gracious generosity, His undeserved favor and spiritual blessing), [in] that though **He was [so very] rich, yet for your sakes He became [so very] poor**, in order that by His poverty you might become enriched (abundantly supplied)."*

Many argue that the word *riches* as used in this scripture, pertains *only* to spiritual wealth and *not* material wealth. This argument cannot be valid because 2 Corinthians 8:9 relates, to a large degree, the idea of giving and how giving results in blessings to the giver and recipient. Please refer back to chapter 8 on giving, for a more detailed discussion on this subject.

GOD GIVES POWER TO GET WEALTH

Deuteronomy 8:18 (AMP)
*"But you shall [earnestly] remember the Lord your God, for it is He Who **gives you power** to get wealth, that He may establish His covenant which He swore to your fathers, as it is this day."*

The question arises as to why God would give you the power to get wealth if He did not want you to have wealth. The answer would have to be, God wants you to have wealth! Let us refer to one other scripture, which indicates that God wants us to have abundance. In Ecclesiastes 5:19, the Bible states:

Ecclesiastes 5:19 (NIV)
"Moreover, when God gives someone wealth and possessions and the ability to enjoy them, to accept their lot and be happy in their toil—this is a gift of God."

So, if you are a child of God, a born-again Believer, God is delighted to see you prosper. He *wants* us to prosper!

Psalm 35:27 (KJV)
"Let them shout for joy and be glad, that favour my righteous

*cause: yea, let them say continually, Let the Lord be magnified, which hath **pleasure in the prosperity of his servant.**"*

WRONG ATTITUDES TOWARD MONEY

God does not get displeased when we obtain prosperity. If He wanted to see us in poverty, He would not have told us that He has pleasure in the prosperity of His servant, Psalm 35:27. God *opposes* pride, arrogance, greed and the evil attitudes that are often associated with wealth and riches. The *love* of money is the *root* of all evil, (1 Timothy 6:10). **Money itself is not the problem!** The problems are the *love* of money and the *greed* for money and the *lust* for money. Some people are reluctant to become rich and are even *fearful* of becoming wealthy. They believe they may falter, backslide and ruin their relationship with God. Material prosperity should be placed in the proper perspective.

~~~~~~~~~~~~~~~~~~~
**God wants you to own money
and *not* for money to own you. He wants us to love people and
use money and *not* for us to use people and love money.**
~~~~~~~~~~~

Of course, *you can* let money rule you. There are many things in life that are valuable and beneficial to us that could also harm us. Let's take a car for example. The car is a great blessing, yet thousands of people get killed in car accidents each year. Does that mean you are not supposed to drive a car? No, of course not!

Vitamins are supposed to be healthy and good for us. Did you know that if you take vitamins improperly, they could be harmful to your health? The sun is supposed to be beneficial for us and boost vitamin D levels. Too much sun though, can burn the skin and may even lead to skin cancer. Almost everything used *improperly* can bring harm.

Just like anything else, money should be viewed in a practical way. Misuse money and it will end up misusing you. Deal with money properly and it will deal with you properly. We should have no fear of money because the Lord has told us He **did not give us a spirit of fear but of power, love and a sound mind**, (2 Timothy 1:7). Through prayer and believing the Word of God, you can overcome all evil that might try to befall you once you become prosperous!

Greater is He (God) that is in you than he (the enemy) that is in the world, (1 John 4:4). So, prayer and God's Word can change all ungodly attitudes toward money. The Word says in John 16:23, whatever we ask the Father in the name of Jesus, He will give it to us. If we ask God to take away wrong attitudes toward money, He will do it for us!

MISCONSTRUED SCRIPTURES

Some people say that if God wants me to prosper, then why are there so many scriptures that seem to imply it is bad to be rich and good to be poor? Below, I will point out certain of the scriptures that are often misunderstood and will provide evidence to *dispel* the notion that the Word advocates we should live in poverty and lack.

THE RICH YOUNG RULER

One story in the Bible that is commonly misunderstood is the one that pertains to the discussion between Jesus and the rich young ruler. Let us look at Luke 18:18-27:

Luke 18:18-27(CEV)

*"An important man asked Jesus, "Good Teacher, what must I do to have eternal life?"¹⁹ Jesus said, "Why do you call me good? Only God is good.²⁰ You know the commandments: 'Be faithful in marriage. Do not murder. Do not steal. Do not tell lies about others. Respect your father and mother.'"²¹ He told Jesus, "I have obeyed all these commandments since I was a young man."²² When Jesus heard this, he said, "There is one thing you still need to do. **Go and sell everything you own! Give the money to the poor** and you will have riches in heaven. Then come and be my follower."*

²³ When the man heard this, he was sad, because he was very rich.²⁴ Jesus saw how sad the man was. So he said, "It's terribly hard for rich people to get into God's kingdom! ²⁵ In fact, it's easier for a camel to go through the eye of a needle than for a rich person to get into God's kingdom."

People have greatly misconstrued these verses. In verse 22, Jesus said, "go and sell everything you own! *Give* the money to the poor." Jesus knew when He made this statement this individual could *not* part with his wealth. The Lord used divine wisdom to show the man his heart. Jesus wanted to show him that *his wealth had a strong grip on him*. The wealth had him in a vice! The lesson we are supposed to learn, *is not* that it is good for us to be poor. It *is not* better to be poor than to be rich. The lesson actually is, ***don't let money rule you.*** Don't let money become your god.

~~~~~~~~~~~~~~~~~~~~~

Unfortunately, many people falsely come to the conclusion that those who are rich cannot be spiritual, holy or committed to God.

~~~~~~~~~~~

The premise that God wants us to be poor runs counter to many scriptures. For now, let me just point out that Jesus said, He came so we might have life and have it more abundantly (John 10:10).

Poverty is not abundant living! If you are unable to pay your electric bill, that is *not* abundant living. If your car gets repossessed, that is *not* abundant living. If you have a toothache and cannot afford to go to the dentist for help, that is *not* abundant living. ***Poverty is not a blessing!*** I repeat poverty is ***not*** a blessing. It is an enemy.

*So, **we should not buy into the unscriptural notion that God wants us to be poor! It is unequivocally untrue!!***

With regard to the story of the rich young ruler, people fail to consider the statements that Jesus made to His followers just after He told the young man to relinquish his wealth. In Luke,

18:27, the Lord said to His followers, "The things, which are impossible with men, are possible with God" (KJV).

Jesus was saying, a man who has wealth and who excludes God from his life is in serious trouble. He points out with *God absent from his life,* a rich man can never overcome the problems, grip and bondage associated with money. Jeremiah 32:17 says nothing is too hard for the Lord. If nothing is too hard for God, then He can convict a rich man to live in a godly manner and not let wealth and riches be his god. The rich person who yields to the Lord can retain wealth and still live a holy and godly life.

Also in the story of the rich young ruler, Jesus also told His disciples anyone who follows Him would be blessed.

Luke 18:29-30 (CEV)
"Jesus answered, "You can be sure that anyone who gives up home or wife or brothers or family or children because of God's kingdom [30] *will be given much more in this life. And in the future world they will have eternal life."*

This promise is relatively clear. If you give up that which is yours to follow the Lord, He will bless you substantially. Had the rich young ruler given up his wealth, the Lord, according to His promise, would have greatly blessed the young man and he would have had the privilege of becoming one of the disciples of Christ.

RICH ZACCHAEUS

Luke 19 tells us that Zacchaeus was a tax collector, who was rich and he wanted to see Jesus as He was passing through. Zacchaeus was short in stature so he could not see Jesus over the crowd and decided to climb up into a tree. Jesus saw him in the tree and told him to come down because He, Jesus, needed to stay at Zacchaeus' house.

Luke 19:7-10 (GW)
*"But the people who saw this began to express disapproval. They said, **"He went to be the guest of a sinner."** [8] Later, at dinner, Zacchaeus stood up and said to the Lord, **"Lord, I'll give half of my property to the poor. I'll pay four times as much as I owe to those I have cheated in any way."** [9] Then Jesus said to Zacchaeus, **"You and your family have been saved today.** You've shown that you, too, are one of Abraham's descendants. [10] Indeed, the Son of Man has come to seek and to save people who are lost."*

Notice the difference in the way Jesus dealt with Zacchaeus in comparison to the way He dealt with the rich young ruler. Jesus told Zacchaeus, who was rich, that salvation had come to his *whole household*. This comment was made *after* Jesus pointed out that Zacchaeus' heart was in the right place and *he was not held in captivity and bondage by money.*

Zacchaeus said he would give half of his money to the poor and he would pay four times as much as he owed those he had cheated in any way. Apparently, at the time he came in contact with Jesus, **he was *not* obsessed with money!**

Another important consideration to take into account is, even if Zacchaeus did follow through on his promise and did in fact giveaway half of his wealth, it is highly doubtful the amount left would have made him poor. In other words a person who gives away one half of a large sum of money will still have a large sum of money left over!

It is also important to note that nowhere in the Word is it recorded that Jesus said to him: yes, Zacchaeus, you are right, go ahead and give away half your money to the poor! Of course, it is good to give to the poor but Jesus apparently was more concerned with his **attitude toward money** than with the fact that he had money.

If Jesus had been more concerned about the mere fact that Zacchaeus was rich, he probably would have told Zacchaeus to go ahead and give to the poor.

The Lord knew a person with a giving heart who was not bound by money would do the right thing and give abundantly. From this we can reasonably conclude that Jesus had no problem with the fact that Zacchaeus had wealth.

Jesus was only concerned that the man had a pure heart and the proper attitude toward money. God is the same yesterday, today and forever (Hebrews 13:8). Accordingly, the Lord has no problem with us having wealth and prosperity today.

WHY GOD WANTS YOU TO HAVE MONEY

By now it should be clear that God wants us to prosper and have money in abundance. We know people desire money for good and evil purposes. Money can be used for godly and ungodly purposes. God wants us to prosper financially but He also wants us to use His wisdom and guidance to properly handle money.

PROVIDING FOR FAMILY

1 Timothy 5:8 (GW)
"If anyone doesn't take care of his own relatives, especially his immediate family, he has denied the Christian faith and is worse than an unbeliever."

It is impossible to provide for your family if you do not have the money to do so. Even if you have *some* money but not sufficient money, you'll still find it difficult, if not impossible, to take care of your family needs. You'll find it really hard to meet this requirement, which is imposed by God. If you don't provide for your own family, you will be a poor advertisement for the gospel of Jesus Christ. More importantly, *it is unscriptural for a person to refuse to provide for his or her own family* as can be gleaned above from 1 Timothy 5:8.

THE ANSWER TO ALL THINGS

The Bible says in Ecclesiastes 10:19, money answereth all things. I do not believe money will directly, answer all things but indirectly it will. For instance, you might say, money will not answer the problems of a person dying from incurable cancer or AIDS. Perhaps money cannot directly heal these diseases but indirectly money *can* heal these diseases! How? They can be healed through the Word of God. The Lord has told us that He heals *all* diseases, (Psalm 103:3). He has also told us that by the stripes of Jesus we are healed, (1 Peter 2:24).

The Word lets us know that divine healing is available to us even for so-called incurable diseases. There is *no problem* that is too big for the Lord to solve. The Lord depends on men and women to tell the world about His Word and all of His wonderful promises such as the promises of divine healing, prosperity, success and peace. The Lord has told us we can do all things through Christ who strengthens us (Philippians 4:13). He has told us whatever we ask the Father in the name of Jesus, He will give it to us, John 16:23.

~~~~~~~~~~~~~~~~~~~~
**Through faith, prayer and the power of God
there is *nothing* that is impossible for us!**
~~~~~~~~~~

Where does the money come in? It costs money to expose the world to the revelation that prayer makes all things possible.

It costs money to buy Bibles to share, so people can learn that all things are possible through faith, prayer and the power of God. It costs money to finance churches where the Word is preached. It costs money to buy a public address system, pews and pulpits and especially the salaries of ministers who teach and preach the gospel.

It costs money to buy airtime to proclaim the Gospel of God. It costs money to host websites to proclaim the Gospel of God. It costs money to host podcasts that proclaim the Gospel of God. It costs money to do these and many other things to proclaim the Gospel of God. And yes, it costs money to *print books* to teach the Gospel of God!

Because money is so instrumental in the propagation of the Gospel, which has the answer to all problems, it can truly be said that money *is* the answer to all things.

ABUNDANT LIFE

The Lord wants us to have abundant life, (John 10:10). It is hard to be happy when there is no abundance. **The Lord does not want us to live in poverty.** He wants us to live happy, joyous and successful lives, (John 15:8).

Money can play a great part in helping us to obtain joy and happiness and success, provided it is viewed and handled in ways that are scriptural and are in line with the Word of God.

13

BE ENCOURAGED!

"Many of life's failures are people who did not realize how close they were to success when they gave up."
–Thomas A. Edison

The success principles I am sharing with you really do work.

How do I know? Because they have worked in my life, as well as the lives of my family, friends and even strangers. I am not sharing something with you that's only theory. I am not sharing something with you that's only religious. I am not sharing something with you that's only hearsay. I know from whence I speak. What I am sharing with you is life changing!

My present life, the success that I have achieved, *is not by accident, it is not by chance and it is not coincidental*. It is because I did what God said to do to be successful. I have experienced the reality of the power in following God's Word to live a successful life.

I have gone from *defeat to success and triumph*. I have gone from *downtroddenness and despair to unspeakable joy and happiness*. Following God's Word has completely changed and turned around my life! What turned on the light bulb for me?

"Blessed is the one who does not walk in step with the wicked or stand in the way that sinners take or sit in the company of mockers but whose delight is in the law of the LORD and who meditates on his law day and night. That person is like a tree planted by streams of water, which yields its fruit in season and whose leaf does not wither – whatever they do prospers."

This is the scripture that got me on the road to success. I had to read it several times before it really sank in but when it did - changes started in my life!

YOU ARE CALLED TO SUCCEED

You and I are *exactly* the same in God's eyes. He loves us all unconditionally. God didn't say, "Oh - there's my son Calvin from Tomlinson Hill, Texas and I'm going to do for him what I won't do for anybody else." NO, that's not how God operates! Everybody has a fair shot at receiving all the benefits that come to those who give their lives to Jesus. Here's the trick, if you don't follow the directions, the plan won't work. God has called *you* to *succeed* but if you don't cooperate by following His Word, you won't experience the benefits! Your commitment to God is imperative.

COMMITMENT IS KEY

Your initial experience with a deep commitment to God will

cause faith to develop within you. Your faith will be growing. You may not be able to see any tangible evidence of change in your life immediately but as with anything, *time* does cause *change* to come.

When you plant seeds in the ground, they start growing underneath the surface of the ground. At first, you will not be able to see *any* evidence of the growth. With the passage of time though, the seeds will sprout and later grow up to be mature plants.

~~~~~~~~~~~~~~~~~~~~
The blessings you desire will not manifest overnight. Stored in your spirit are years of doubt, disappointment and unbelief.
~~~~~~~~~~~

It took some time for you to become that way. So, likewise, it will take some time for the water of God's Word to wash away the negative effects of these deeply rooted attitudes and beliefs.

DETERMINATION IS KEY

**"You can never cross the ocean
until you have the courage to lose sight of the shore."
–Christopher Columbus**

When I was in law school, I would in effect, *memorize* some law books in preparation for final exams. I would study 10-12 hours nonstop sometimes. That is the type of dogged determination I had to have to get through law school. It paid off! This zeal and determination that I had to get through law school has been transferred to a zeal and determination for the things of God.

Why? Because I answered God's call for me to succeed in life! Yet, there are many people who believe they can pray to God five minutes a day and lead a victorious and successful life. God is no respecter of persons but He is a rewarder of those who diligently seek Him.

DILIGENTLY SEEK GOD

"The elevator to success is out of order.
You have to use the stairs. One step at a time."
-Unknown

The words *diligently seek,* mean you should pursue God in a way that you never have before. I want you to be successful in life through Jesus Christ. There are some successful people in the world from whom we can gain some pointers. I am partial to athletics and have closely observed the diligence that superstars have employed to succeed.

"Diligence, the one virtue
that embraces in it, all the rest."
-Roman Proverb

PERSISTENCE IS KEY

"Our motto must continue to be perseverance. And ultimately I trust the Almighty will crown our efforts with success."
-William Wilberforce

One very famous football player persistently pursues success. He does one particular exercise several thousand times each day. That is only one of his many routine exercises and he does it thousands of times, at a time! That is how he stays in shape. He knows his physical fitness is critical and crucial to his success.

Another famous athlete, a basketball star, has the same type of drive. He practices sharpening his shooting skills several hours every night. He shoots the ball several thousand times on most days. This is *along with* his team's regularly scheduled practice. He is one of the top players in his field. Then consider the courage, tenacity and dedication of the man who climbed Mount Everest (the world's tallest mountain) at 80 years old. What a remarkable and noteworthy feat!

If these people can pursue secular goals with such resolve and achieve international acclaim and notoriety, why can't Believers in God seek Him with the same kind of intensity? I have fasted on many occasions but on one occasion I went on a 40 day fast. It was very difficult but worth the effort. I was able to successfully get a number of revelations from God!

Some may call it *insanity* but then, they may not have the revelation that *they* are **CALLED TO SUCCEED**.

YOU THINK YOU'RE FAILING?

"Men were born to succeed not fail."
– Henry David Thoreau

Just because you aren't able to achieve your dreams yet, doesn't mean that your life is over. Sometimes we think we need one particular thing to make us happy and we forget all the other things that make us happy. If one dream doesn't work out, find a new one! Jeremiah was an absolute failure when judged by people's definition of success. For many years he served as God's representative but when he spoke no one listened or responded.

His neighbors, his family, the priests and prophets, friends, his audiences and the kings *all* rejected him. He was poor and underwent severe deprivation to deliver God's messages. He was thrown into prison and into a cistern. But in God's eyes he was a success. He faithfully and courageously proclaimed God's Word and His messages and he was obedient to his calling.

"I have not failed.
I've just found 10,000 ways that won't work."
-Thomas A. Edison

"The people who succeed the most are the people who have failed the most, because they are people who have tried the most."
-Anonymous

PASSION FOR SUCCESS

"If opportunity doesn't knock, build a door."
-Unknown

Your passions are the pipelines to your soul. When you are connected to your passions, you feel happy, self-motivated, fulfilled, engaged and worthwhile. When you are disconnected from your true purpose, you become unhappy and ultimately depressed.

CHANGE OR STAY THE SAME

"Don't dream of success, wake up and achieve it."
-Anonymous

Everybody's life is different. You may not have to pursue God as much as I did to get out of a tormented life, like me. You might not have to put in as much work as some high profile athletes. But you might have to pursue God **more** than you have done until now. That is, *if* you want to see a change in your life and live like you received God's call for you to succeed!

So what can you do? *Get spiritually radical!* Remember the $600 million dollar lottery? Even people that don't play the lottery did that one time! Why? They got caught up in all the craze of the possibility of winning all that money! The country got lottery radical!

That kind of frenzy is what I've been giving to God since I realized He called me to succeed. I got spiritually active, just like the superstar athletes got physically active! I wanted all my blessings that had been stolen and kept from me by my ignorance and the devil's arrogance! God has already done His part by sending Jesus to die on the cross for us. Now, it's our time to do our part. God has already called us to success, the question is - will you answer, YES?

"Ninety-nine percent of all failures come from people who have a habit of making excuses."
-George Washington Carver

Show the world and the devil that we are more than conquerors in Christ. Walk in boldness. TIME IS OF THE ESSENCE! Get actively involved in changing your life from where it is now, to what it can be.

SPEAK LIFE TO YOUR LIFE

"It is hard to fail but it is worse never to have tried to succeed."
-Theodore Roosevelt

I want you to do this! The following faith talk will change your life. The *more* times you say it, the *less* time it will take to see a manifestation of change in your life. The *fewer* times you say it, the *more* time it will take to see the manifestation. If you only say it once or twice a day...get ready to wait. If you're like me and speak the Word thousands of times a day, get ready to see results!

Speak the following words as often as you can. *Memorize it.* Say it in the car, traveling, on vacation, in the bathtub, shower or wherever you have some private space. It doesn't matter if you're cooking, cleaning or working! Just say it, say it and say it again! Say this out loud or silently to yourself many times a day:

#1 Thank You God for giving me Your favor, Your peace, great health and success, at all that I do.

#2 Thank You God for making me a great financial success and a person whose needs are met by the power of Almighty God.

14

TAKE ACTION

"One and God make a majority."
-Frederick Douglass

The purpose of this book is to enlighten you as to what might possibly be blocking the success God has promised in your life. Just reading these pages will do little for you. It is time now for you to *take action*. God has given us a plan of action through His Word. The Word is the blueprint for our lives.

Accordingly, this book contains many scriptures but in order for these scriptures to change your life, you must take action. You must pray, change your heart; change your mindset and beliefs. You must move on in the Lord. If what you have been doing has not worked, then you need to change.

This book is designed to help you change. This chapter is totally dedicated to action. This is your opportunity to do something, in line with the Word, to change your circumstances.

To be successful in this endeavor, you *must not allow doubt* to enter into the picture. Belief and pure trust in the Lord Jesus Christ is a must. To ponder, wonder, philosophize and theorize will simply postpone your desired result. This chapter is not a magical formula but a standard for you to operate by for the rest of your life. You may truly be able to change the course of your life in employing the principles and strategies set forth in the following pages. God's Word is *truth*. His principles produce *life*.

I know what it's like to be stressed out by bills and *not* have enough money to pay them. I know what it's like to want a promotion and can't get it. I know what it's like to be betrayed by a friend.

I know what it's like to have your good, well-intentioned actions talked about negatively. I know what it's like to have absolutely nobody to turn to for help. I have been intimately acquainted with these and so much more. I have been there!

**"When you can do the common things of life
in an uncommon way,
you will command the attention of the world."
-George Washington Carver**

So whatever situation you are in, I can probably relate to it. I took action to get free from the enemy's trap. I pray you take the same action and are blessed.

PRAYER FOR GENERAL SUCCESS IN LIFE

The substitutionary work of Jesus gives us the potential to obtain eternal life. The work of Jesus also gives us the capability of living lives full of victory, abundance and success overall. However, we still have to ask the Lord to give us the blessings He has promised us. To operate in overall success, triumph and abundance in life, pray this prayer:

Lord, Your Word says that Jesus came so that we may have life and have it more abundantly. It further says that if we are doers of Your Word that we would be blessed in our deeds. It is Your will Lord that we be blessed in the city, in the country, coming in, going out and blessed at all that we set our hands unto. Lord, I follow Your Word and I ask that You fulfill these promises in my life. I earnestly ask You Lord to give me Your favor, mercy, grace and success in all aspects of my life. In the mighty name of Jesus I pray. Amen.

PRAYER FOR REMOVAL OF
SPIRITUAL BLOCKERS TO SUCCESS

Many of the conditions, obstacles and barriers to our success have been erected through negative words that have flowed from our mouths. That which has been erected through errant, ungodly and negative speech can be dismantled, pulled down or destroyed the same way – through the words from the mouth. Say this:

The name of Jesus is above every name. I use the name of Jesus to pull down strongholds, obstacles, setbacks and barriers that have blocked me from being as successful as God desires. I command every weight, burden, hardship and struggle to depart from me now, in the powerful name of Jesus. Failure, sickness, defeat and lack, go from my life right now in the mighty name of Jesus. I call myself free of hindrances, obstacles and barriers to success in the name of Jesus Christ. I call myself strong in the Lord and in the power of His might. In the matchless name of Jesus. Amen.

PRAYER TO OPERATE
IN DEDICATION AND TENACITY

We may sometimes become tired and weak and thus fail to move forward in pursuit of God and our goals. Always remember, God rewards those who diligently seek Him. We should likewise remember we *must not be weary* in well doing and we will reap a great harvest if we don't give up. To get help from God, to pursue Him, your goals and dreams, pray the prayer below:

Lord, You said that Your Word is a lamp unto my feet and a light unto my path. You also said that You are my fortress, stronghold, my loving God, my Hightower, my

shield and my strength. Teach me and empower me dear God, to diligently and tenaciously fight the good fight of faith. Give me strength and enablement and ability to press on toward the goal to win the prize that God's heavenly call offers in Christ Jesus. Help me now dear Lord to never give up but to endure and stay diligent and committed to You until the end. In the name of Jesus. Amen.

PRAYER TO MATURE IN THE LORD

In order for us to be better used by God, we must get closer to Him. The Lord won't do very much through a person who is not very dedicated to Him. We are supposed to love the Lord with all our hearts and strongly commit to Him. To get closer to God, pray this prayer:

Lord Your Word says, that I am supposed to love You with all my heart, soul, strength and mind. Dear Lord, I love You with all my heart, soul, strength and mind and submit myself to You, totally and completely. You said that if I draw near to You that You would draw near to me. I seek You Lord and draw near to You. I believe that, in return, You are drawing closer to me. As I grow closer to You and You grow closer to me God, I make myself available body, soul and spirit to be used more and more by You. Help me to mature so that I can capably and effectively respond to the call You have on my life. Teach me to daily walk in wisdom, great divine favor and great spiritual knowledge, understanding and maturity. In the name of Jesus I pray. Amen.

PRAYER FOR FORGIVENESS

If there is the most *remote* possibility you may not have forgiven someone who has done any wrong to you, whether they are alive or dead, you *must* ask God to forgive you and you *must* forgive and release that person or persons. Pray this prayer out loud:

Father God, I thank You that I have been purchased by the blood of Jesus. I come before You and I confess that I have held unforgiveness in my heart. I say that this is sin and I am repentant for it. I know Your Word says that if I do not forgive, You will not forgive me. As an act of my free will and not my emotions, I choose to forgive each and every person who has hurt me, abused me, mistreated me, lied on me, embarrassed me, rejected me, betrayed me, stolen from me or done any wrong to me in anyway over the span of my life. (Here, name every person that may be in this category whether alive or deceased. Write down a list if you need to). God, I choose to forgive _____ and _____ etc. and anyone else that I can't remember, now. In the mighty name of Jesus.

PRAYER ABOUT UNFORGIVENESS

I release *all unforgiveness* that I have held in my heart against each person just named now. I break covenant with unforgiveness and its power over my heart. I walk in repentance before You, Father and now ask You to forgive me. I have fallen short of the glory of God but I receive Your forgiveness of my sin, whereby I can again come to Your throne of grace in my time of need. I thank You Father. In the name of Jesus. Amen.

PRAYER FOR GOD'S
CONTROL OVER YOUR FINANCES

The world will tell you, "Pick yourself up by your own bootstraps." The enemy will tell you, "You don't need anyone but yourself to make it big in life." Your pride will tell you, "I've got all the answers!" All of these statements are *contrary* to the Word of God. If you have held these beliefs, you have tried to operate in your own strength. To operate in God's strength, pray this prayer out loud:

Father God, I give up! I have tried to be a success in this world according to the dictates and standards of this world. I have kept You out of my finances. I have trusted in man and myself but not in You. Forgive me for the error of my ways, Lord. I know that Your Word says I am not supposed to rely on my own abilities. I ask You Lord, to help me change my thoughts and my heart so that I can submit my finances to You. I ask You God, to be Lord over my finances. I release all control over my money to You. Thank You Father. In the name of Jesus. Amen.

PRAYER FOR BREAKING WORD TRAPS

If you feel there may be word traps that are blocking your success and are keeping you in bondage, pray this prayer aloud. Remember, word traps can come from enemies, family, friends and even yourself!

Father God, I thank You for the ability to break the power of evil words spoken against me and my life by my words or the words of others. I now break the power of every word trap that has held me in bondage-spiritually, physically, financially, socially or emotionally. I remove and destroy the power of all words operating against my life, which includes words from my childhood, my parents, psychics, acquaintances, those in authority or anyone else I may have submitted my life to. I renounce and cancel each and every word spoken against me that is not in line with the Word of God. I break the power of every word spoken against me to intentionally or unintentionally inflict harm on my life. I break and cancel the power of all evil and negative words spoken against me jokingly or in jest. I command all ungodly words to release their hold over my life, my success and my future now. In the name of Jesus. Amen.

PRAYER FOR BREAKING ANCESTRAL CURSES

You have no control over what your ancestors did. The Bible says the sins of the fathers are passed down to the third and fourth generations (Exodus 20:5). You are reaping the result of their actions whether good or bad, blessings or curses. Why take the *chance* of not breaking away from any ancestral curses that *may be* in your bloodline? Pray this prayer aloud:

Father, I thank You and praise You for the redemptive work of Jesus on Calvary. Jesus became a curse for me by hanging on the tree (cross). Father, Your Word says that the iniquity (sins) of the fathers (my ancestors) will visit (be cast on) the third and fourth generations (Exodus 20:5). I repent for any of my sins or the sins of my ancestors that have come upon my life to cause hardships and problems. I repent for the sins of their participation or my participation in the occult, witchcraft, astrology, satan worship or any other hidden or mysterious supernatural actions. I renounce all of these and confess them as sin and an abomination to God. I also renounce, (here, call out anything such as illegal drug sales, robbery or stealing that you or your ancestors have done). I ask Your forgiveness Father for any known or unknown sins on both sides of my family back ten generations. I break the power of each curse passed on to

me through the sins of my ancestors. I appropriate the blood of Jesus to ancestral sins and my personal sins. I renounce, break and loose from me and my family, the power of each ancestral curse. In the name of Jesus. Amen.

PRAYER FOR BREAKING JUDGMENTS

Again, whether you are *aware* or *unaware* of it, you have made judgments. These judgments should be cancelled or broken. Pray this prayer aloud:

Father, Your Word says to judge not. I confess that I have made ungodly judgments of others. I have spoken ill of others and have interjected my own scorn of them or of their actions. I ask You to forgive me of this Lord. I have gone against Your Word. I ask You to forgive me of all ungodly judgments of my father, mother, sister, brother, extended relatives, friends, Pastor or fellow Believers. Father, forgive me for judging others as poor, stingy, tightfisted, incompetent, inferior, never able to make ends meet, dumb and stupid. I break such judgments that I have made. I loose and free myself, family and friends from the power of these judgments. I also loose and free the lives of the people I have judged. I cancel and break the power and effect of every judgment operating to cause harm to me or my household now, in the name of Jesus. Amen.

PRAYER FOR FINANCIAL BLESSING

Father God, I come before You in the name of Jesus and ask You to forgive me of any sin I have committed, known or unknown. I know by Your Word that whatever I ask for in the name of Jesus, You will give me. I receive Your forgiveness and can now stand boldly before Your throne of grace in my time of need. Father, I thank You and praise You that Jesus was made a curse for me by hanging on the tree (cross). I am redeemed from the curse of poverty and the blessings of Abraham have come upon me through Jesus Christ. Lord I choose to seek first the kingdom of God and Your righteousness and according to Your Word, You will meet all of my needs according to Your riches in glory by Jesus Christ. I thank You and praise You Lord that I am prosperous because you desire above all things that I prosper and be in health as my soul prospers. Lord, because I have given my life to You, I am your servant; therefore You take pleasure in my prosperity and Your blessing makes me rich and You add no sorrow with it. I obey You Lord and serve You, so I will spend my days in prosperity and my years in pleasure and joy. I am grateful to You Father, that although Jesus was rich, He became poor for my sake that I through His poverty might become rich. Because I bring all my tithes and offerings into the church and to Your ministries to help spread the gospel of Jesus, You open the windows of heaven to me and pour out blessings abundantly on me, so much that I don't have enough room to receive them all. I thank You for manifesting financial blessings in my life. In the name of Jesus I pray. Amen.

PRAYER TO CHANGE YOUR MIND

One of the main challenges to overcome when trying to become successful is the weight or hindrance of thinking poorly or negatively of *yourself*. If you have been seeing yourself as inferior, a failure, no good, worthless or useless because of your background or current situation, you should read this prayer aloud daily:

Father, Your Word says that I have the mind of Christ. I know that Jesus is not impoverished, inadequate or second rate. Jesus is not worthless or useless. Lord, because I have the mind of Christ, I choose not to receive thoughts about myself that are not in line with Your Word. Father God, I trust you with all my heart. I do not trust in money, riches or the wealth of the world but in You only. As I acknowledge You God in all my ways, You shall direct my path, my life and my success. You discern the thoughts and intentions of my heart. I choose to not think evil thoughts but to think on those things which are true, honest, just, pure, lovely and of good report. I know that the weapons of our warfare are not carnal but are mighty through God to the pulling down of ungodly thoughts such as thoughts of worthlessness, failure, uselessness, inferiority and poverty. I cast down these five imaginations because they exalt themselves against the knowledge of God and I bring into captivity every thought to the obedience of Christ. I am not conformed to thoughts about myself that are ungodly but I am transformed by the renewing of my mind. Father, from this day forward, I commit my works unto You and my thoughts are established by You according to Your perfect will for my life. In the name of Jesus. Amen.

WARNING! WARNING! WARNING!

The prayers that you have just prayed are just like hitting a concrete wall with a sledgehammer. One strike won't demolish the wall. Maybe you'll get a crack started. The more you hit the wall, the weaker it becomes. Keep hitting and the concrete starts chipping away. Keep at it and the wall gets weaker and weaker until ultimately, it gives way and no longer serves its purpose as a wall.

So it goes with the walls that are in your life keeping you from success. The more you strike the wall with these prayers, the weaker the walls become. Keep at it and no power of hell can stop, block or keep you from the success God has called you to experience in this life. The more you pray, the weaker the walls become.

~~~~~~~~~~~~~~~~~~~~~

Once the walls crumble, prepare for the tsunami of blessings that will flood your life!

~~~~~~~~~~

Actual cotton field Calvin Washington visited years later.

15

EVERYBODY'S GOT
A COTTON FIELD

**"Troubles are often the tools by which
God fashions us for better things."
-Henry Ward Beecher**

Inasmuch as most people are unfamiliar with the drudgery
(tedious, menial, hard, monotonous routine work) of picking
cotton as a child of the 50's and 60's, let me take you on a
journey of what it was like. Picking cotton is literally picking
the soft lightweight cotton out of the hard razor sharp boll.
Pulling cotton is the removal of the entire boll from the cotton
stalk. We did both. It all depended on what method the "Boss
Man" wanted. To make things simple, both methods of work
were just called "picking cotton."

The day always started early; around 5 or 6 a.m. Before
daybreak, we would get up eat, get dressed and wait for the
"contractor or Boss Man" to pick us up. We rode to the field in
the back of a homemade truck bed with a tarp covering and a
trailer hitched up to it. The truck would make several stops
picking up "hands" along the way. It would be so crowded

with 12-15 people; we would be *packed together* like sardines in a can. Each day we went to the field it was *extremely important* that we bring certain essential items:

1. **A heavy canvas sack** with a strap that went over the shoulder and was about 10 to 12 feet long. The sacks often developed large holes in the bottom as a result of being dragged through the dirt in the fields for many miles. Some people couldn't afford to buy a new sack, so they would patch the old one. Some sacks were patched so much they resembled patchwork quilts.

2. **A large straw hat** to provide sufficient protection of the head and face from the brutal Texas sun.

3. **A long sleeved shirt** to protect the arms from the sun and the bolls (protective covering) of the cotton plant.

4. **A water cup** to avoid drinking after other people and catching their germs. A water cooler was provided on the contractor truck or under the trailer.

5. **Cotton gloves**, especially for women. The gloves served to protect against cuts, scrapes and scratches that came from the hard, sharp pointed edged boll. The edges were as sharp as razors. I usually didn't wear gloves because they slowed me down, reduced my productivity and my earnings overall. As a result, my hands were always rough, cut, scarred, scratched up and *often bloody.*

6. **Knee pads**. Some people resorted to picking cotton while crawling on their knees (*on top of rocks, etc.*) once the pain from bending their back became too intense and unbearable. Most

of the plants were no more than 1-2 feet high, so bending was mandatory for most. I tried to stay away from crawling, in spite of the excruciating back pain, so I could move faster through the field to earn more money. Sometimes my back would hurt so badly I would have to give in and crawl on my knees just like the others but *without* the benefit of knee pads. Crawling across sharp edged rocks was *excruciating!*

7. **A very hefty lunch**. Lunches usually consisted of, luncheon meats like summer sausage, bologna, liver loaf (we called it goose liver), cookies, fruit or leftovers from the prior night's dinner. It took a great deal of energy and strength to drag the heavy 10-12 foot cotton sack through the field, carry it back to the trailer, lift it high enough to toss it on the inside of the trailer and then empty it.

8. **A little money**. The contractor would often ask the workers if they wanted him go to the store. He would take requests to make a run for snacks, chips and sodas, etc.

Without these essentials, the day in the field would have been intolerable. To save time and earn more money, the more dedicated workers would never make a special trip to the trailer to get water. They felt this would take up too much time. They would only get water when they went to the trailer to weigh and empty the cotton sack. The more committed workers would not talk very much because they felt talking was a distraction that would waste a great deal of time.

On a rare occasion we would be able to find a shade tree at the end of the field to eat lunch. On most days though, the low-lying cotton trailer served as the only place to protect us from the sun as we ate lunch. I hated lunchtime. *We would have to crawl on the ground to get under the trailer.* Since the trailer was only about two feet off the ground, there was not enough space to sit under it. We would have to lie on our stomachs or backs and eat on the ground. It reminded me of how Frisco, our dog, would crawl under the house to get away from the sun. That's what lunchtime did for me; *made me feel like a dog. Even more heartbreaking, was to see my mother and grandmother crawl under the trailer too.*

The temperature in the field was usually in the upper nineties and sometimes it exceeded 100 degrees. I used to feel so badly for my brother Earl. The sun and other bad conditions were not all that oppressed him. He was allergic to the insecticide spray used to kill boll weevils. He would have reactions similar to asthmatic attacks. He would keep on pushing in spite of this problem.

THE CONTRACTOR & "BOSS MAN"

The contractor was the man who would locate the cotton crop. The landowner ("Boss Man") would make the work available for us (the "hands"). I used to pray for rain so I would not have to see the contractor, his truck, the cotton field or the hot Texas sun. The rain almost never came. We even picked cotton on Labor Day. I remember one Labor Day in particular, when the contractor didn't show up because rain was in the forecast and there was a light shower around the time we would normally be picked up.

MY HERO VISITS

I was about thirteen or fourteen at the time. My eldest brother Malfred was visiting us from Odessa, Texas, which is several hundred miles away from where we lived. He was and still is our hero! When Malfred came to visit us, it was like Christmas in the summer, spring or fall. He had a beautiful new *air-conditioned* car. You have to understand, in those days in Tomlinson Hill, new cars were a rarity, especially *air-conditioned* ones. My brother would ride us all around central Texas in his new car. Sometimes he would even take us to the big city of San Antonio, which is almost two hundred miles away.

THE "TUB"

My brother would almost always take us to Waco and other neighboring towns. He would buy us fruit, candy, cake, ice cream and tons of other food. He would often take us to a well-known, somewhat historical eatery in nearby Marlin, called the "Tub." Marlin is the county seat of Falls County and is only about 6 miles from Tomlinson Hill. The Tub is a unique place.

At this locally famous eatery, various types of meats were

thrown altogether and cooked at one time with a dark liquid in a container that resembled a huge tin tub. That's how it got the name the "Tub." People came from near and far to get food from the famous Tub. Even today, I still go by to see the owner when I am in Marlin. I have tried *so many times* to introduce my wife to the culinary delights of the Tub but once she saw it, she *refused* to eat from the "Tub."

FUN IN FALLS COUNTY

Malfred would sometimes take us to the mineral well in Marlin and we would drink naturally hot mineral water, supposedly for its medicinal value. The mineral well was famous also. In the summer, he would even take us to a place just outside of Marlin called the "Falls" of the Brazos River, the longest river in Texas.

The Falls of the Brazos is a county park where people bring recreational vehicles, have picnics and wade and swim in the water. The Falls itself consists of a long slab of cement left from an old bridge that goes from one side of the river to the other.

The slab of cement makes the river look and act like a waterfall. People come from miles to enjoy this park, especially during the summer. That was always a good place for us to go to have a *great* time.

DISAPPOINTMENT OVERWHELMED ME

I had this excitement pent up in me and I looked forward to that Labor Day. The rain had to be *heavy*, really, really *heavy*, to stop us from picking cotton. As I watched the light rain, I longed and yearned for it to continue and get more intense. After all, Malfred, my hero was in town visiting us! As time passed, the rain began to get slower and slower until it stopped. I suppose the drizzle stopped around 9:00 a.m., long after the "hands" would normally have been picked up. At about 10:00 a.m. there was still no sign of the contractor. I was still excited. Then 11:00 a.m. came and there was *still no sign* of the contractor!

I felt happy, joyous and safe at that point. I *couldn't wait* to ride in Malfred's new air-conditioned car and go to Marlin and Waco and get all the goodies we normally got. Then 11:15 a.m. came and the contractor still had not shown up. I thought to myself, "I've got it made now. He's *not* coming!" Then at about 11:30 a.m., my heart sank. The contractor, much to my anger, disappointment and chagrin showed up on the scene. I was floored, brokenhearted and taken aback. Given that I was only thirteen or fourteen, the tears began to freely fall from my eyes. I wanted the rain to fall hard on central Texas and it did not!

On that day (Labor Day) more so than ever, I particularly didn't want to be bothered with cotton, the heartaches and backaches it brought and the unforgiving central Texas sun. I felt like I was being tormented.

OFF TO THE COTTON FIELD

So, we went on to the cotton field, where we would have to bend over almost non-stop, to pick *thousands and thousands* of bolls of cotton. Each boll weighed no more than half an ounce, about the weight of a packet of single serve sugar. The work was *so* repetitive. We had to throw boll, after boll, after boll, in a cotton sack. After throwing hundreds and hundreds of bolls of cotton into the sack, the weight of the sack would *slowly* increase.

It would increase from almost no weight to 1 pound, slowly to 5 pounds, then 15 pounds and then 50 pounds. While continually placing cotton in the sack, we would all have to deal with and get adjusted to the ever increasing, shifting weight of the sack being slowly dragged along the rows of cotton.

Sometime the weight would increase to over 100 pounds as I continually dragged the sack through the field from one end of the row to the other. Once filled, the sack had to be carried (or dragged) to the trailer to be weighed and emptied. The contractor or his wife would have to remain at the trailer at all times because people would carry the sacks of cotton to the trailer at various times throughout the day.

HOW BIG WAS MY COTTON FIELD?

Both the hand and the contractor or his wife would have to keep track of how much cotton was picked (weight) throughout the week. They would have to make sure their records were consistent. I still have one of the little notebooks my father used to keep track of the weight of the cotton he picked. I tear up even now whenever I look at it.

The rows seemed to be unending. To give you an idea, some rows would be about 2 football fields in length and some rows *seemed* to be up to 20 football fields! You had to be wise when considering the direction in which to move throughout the field. I remember making the *terrible* mistake of picking cotton on a very long row and continually moving farther and farther *away* from the trailer as I picked the cotton. This caused me to end up with a *full* sack of cotton after getting to the distance of about 12 to 15 football fields *away* from the trailer.

This prolonged a long painful walk to the trailer with a long heavy sack on my back and shoulder. The key was to pick the cotton and while doing so, move *closer* to the trailer. That way you would have to drag or carry the 100-pound sack only a few feet or few yards. Imagine having to carry a cumbersome cotton sack (on a back already in pain from continual bending) the distance of 12 to 15 football fields! I *quickly* learned how to use better judgment. The key was to pick the cotton and drag the sack so it was being filled as you moved closer and closer *toward* the trailer.

COOPERATION HELPS

Because picking cotton is so labor intensive, husbands and wives would often cooperate by allowing the husband to carry the wife's heavy sack to the trailer for weighing and emptying. After the husband carried his sack to the trailer, he would then return to his wife, get her sack and then take hers to the trailer, as she worked non-stop, by filling his recently emptied sack. My father would often do this for my mother.

EXPERTS KNOW HOW IT'S DONE

Many people became experts at picking cotton. The faster and more proficiently you moved through the field, the more money you could make. My father and my siblings were relatively good at picking cotton. My brother Malfred said he would always focus on the money that could be made. This is how he got his encouragement to work hard. The pay was like 15¢ per pound. So an average person could earn $5.00-$6.00 in a *sun up to sun down* workday.

Some people were like cotton-picking superstars. Even though it was menial labor, those who worked extremely hard, made decent money from picking cotton. I had cousins who picked cotton so well; they earned thousands of dollars a season, picking cotton. They bought new cars and always lived better than others, even then. At first, I was not very good *but I soon caught on.*

LET THE RHYTHM MOVE YOU

After suffering and agonizing over the misery of picking cotton, I learned that it was better mentally and emotionally to work in a rhythm. I also learned to use the rhythm to "attack" the cotton to keep a positive state of mind. The rhythm was almost like dancing, typing or playing a piano. I once read the key to typing was to use a rhythm. I *used the rhythm* in both typing and picking cotton.

In fact I got so good at using the rhythm in typing, I became the Texas statewide typing champion in my school division! It felt great being the state champion. I used to see people in my school break down and cry because they couldn't type as fast and accurately as me. I suspect they couldn't because they didn't know how to get into the rhythm I read about. The rhythm did move me, on the typewriter and in the field.

~~~~~~~~~~~~~~~~~~~~~
If a person would play around and waste time in the cotton field, all they did was prolong the agony and limit their earnings. I refused to play around.
~~~~~~~~~~~

TALKING TO MYSELF

I entered into a mental battle with cotton and poverty like people do when they attempt to climb Mount Everest. I would always fervently say to myself,

~~~~~~~~~~~~~~~~~~~~~~
"Cotton you can't beat me! I will never give up! No poverty, you can't hold me back! I'm going to win poverty and cotton! I'm going to win! I'm gonna be somebody cotton! You can't stop me poverty and cotton! I don't care how much my back hurts and I don't care how hot this sun is or how much my hands bleed! You can't keep me down poverty and cotton! I'm tougher than you cotton! I'm going to go places in life."
~~~~~~~~~~~

I did this to gain encouragement, strength, drive and the will to conquer the cotton and poverty. I felt that if I could conquer cotton, I could conquer other storms in life (hardships, burdens and obstacles). I found a way to cope.

SUPERSTAR IN THE COTTON FIELD

My father, Patrick Henry Washington, told me an inspirational story about a cousin. He said a cousin wanted to pick 1,000 pounds of cotton in 1 day. People would go a whole *lifetime* and were never able to pick a 1,000 pounds of cotton in 1 day, maybe a week but *never* 1 day. *Very few* people could do that, maybe a fraction of 1%. What was even more amazing was that my cousin said he wanted to actually do it, in *half* a day because he wanted to take off early on his birthday. **This was self-inflicted torture!**

Did he go home early on his birthday? Yes, he did! He picked 1,000 pounds in a half day! This was *incredible*. It was like running *20 miles* in *one hour*. It could be compared to one man fighting 10 men and winning the fight. I asked my father how my cousin was able to do that. Daddy said he picked cotton like he was *a wild man*.

My daddy told me the man took *no breaks* and when he carried the heavy sack to the truck, he would literally *run* with it. Then he would run back to the field to quickly continue the work. My father said the man would say something like a chant. He said the man would say while panting and out of breath, "I'm gonna get it cousin Pat, gonna get it, gonna get it. I'm gonna get that thousand. I'm gonna get it cousin Pat, gonna get it, gonna get it" over and over.

Other than that, there was no talking. His behavior could be compared to racecar drivers in a pit stop. There was no delaying. He reached his goal and pulled 1,000 pounds of cotton by noon. What an accomplishment! What a work ethic! People who worked like cotton-picking machines made better money, whereas those who didn't only made meager wages.

LIVING IN A BARN WITH STRANGERS

Although my family picked a great deal of cotton in central Texas, the work was not just limited to our local area. In the early summer, my family would pack up and go to the Corpus Christi area in south Texas.

The living conditions on the trips to south Texas were *far worse* than those at home. Once we got to the land where the cotton was for us to pick, we had to live in an open barn with other families, similar to military barracks. People had to string up sheets to partition off their part of the barn to have privacy to change clothes. Because there were no kitchens or stoves to cook on, people mostly ate out of cans. The shower was in the open air with water from a modified hosepipe behind a few pieces of wood for privacy. The water did have two temperature settings: COLD and VERY COLD.

INFLUENCED BY MY PARENTS

I was greatly influenced by my parents. They were very hard working people. They were also very honest and moral. In the cotton field some people would use tricks to get their sacks of cotton to weigh more than they were supposed to weigh. Some people would throw dirt and rocks in the sack, along with the cotton. Rocks and dirt would produce fake cotton weight. We would get paid based on weight.

This dishonesty caused them to get money they didn't honestly earn. They were supposed to get paid for picking cotton, not for dirt and rocks. Patrick and Inez Washington instilled great moral values in us. My father and mother read us the proverbial "RIOT ACT." My parents told us they had better NOT EVER hear of us engaging in that type of crooked and dishonest behavior. Believe me, we were *afraid* to go against what they told us.

Speaking of honesty, I remember some people had a legal problem involving money. To get these people out of trouble, all my father and mother had to do was *tell a lie and sign some papers*. No one would ever *know about the lie*. The people pleaded with my parents to falsify the papers. Those people might as well have been pleading with our dog, Frisco. My parents basically said, "forget it people."

In fact, they always paid their bills and never had any problems with creditors. I remember one time they bought a car that was a "lemon." They had to make monthly payments on the car loan. Sometime after getting the car, the engine locked making the car worthless.

Even though the car was not drivable, my parents continued to pay off the debt. They had to get another car on credit even though they could barely afford to pay for the car that was the "lemon." This put us in a great financial bind but my parents wanted to be responsible, honest and moral. They paid on both cars at the same time, until they both were paid off.

VALUES LEARNED

My parents taught me values to display in the cotton field and life in general. Sometimes I would complain to them and tell them I was weak or deficient in certain areas of life. I would say things like, "Mother I can never be as smart as the President of the United States or the Governor of Texas." Or I might say, "My buddy can pick cotton much better than I can." She would emphatically say,

"SON THOSE PEOPLE AIN'T NO BETTER THAN YOU!"
-Alma Inez Lewis Washington

When I was in high school, I played basketball on the high school team. One day I was complaining to my father about how great the kids from the larger and better-equipped schools were in basketball. I told my father we couldn't compete with those schools because our school was too small with too many limitations and needs. I was saying we would probably lose almost all of our games. Then from my father, who was not highly educated, came wisdom for the ages. He said,

"WHAT'S WRONG WITH YOU? YOU GOT TWO HANDS AND TWO FOOTS JUST LIKE THEY GOT!"
-Patrick Henry Washington

These words rang in my ears then and stick with me to this day. They rang in my ears when I saw people do better than me in the cotton field. They rang in my ears when I compared myself to others around me, when I was in college, in the army, in law school, when I took the bar exam, when I argued cases in court and when I had problems on my job. The words of my mother and father would *always* come back to my mind when I hit the brick walls of life.

They told me the same thing but in different ways: *"they ain't no better than you"* and *"you got two hands and two foots just like they got."* These words from my parents pushed me to achieve and succeed in life. Thank God for my parents!

WHAT'S YOUR COTTON FIELD?

Many people who read this chapter may feel they are unable to identify with the toils and drudgery of picking cotton.

"Smooth seas do not make skillful sailors."
-African Proverb

Well, everyone can relate to the cotton field if they would just do a quick comparison. The cotton field that was *literal* for me could be *figurative* for everybody else. The cotton field was my source of physical pain, mental torture, depression and was the symbol of economic oppression. So what is the situation in your life that equates to the literal version of the cotton field?

It may not be necessary for you to think too long for your answer. Every person alive has had to deal with something they have hated in life. Whatever has been the source of problems in your life (hardships, troubles, burdens or struggles) can be compared or analogized to the cotton field.

~~~~~~~~~~~~~~~~~~~~~~
The cotton field is a symbol of obstacles and barriers we have a hard time overcoming in life.
~~~~~~~~~~~

For some, the cotton field may be a child who was born with unusually special needs that require a great deal of money, time and attention. It could be a bad marriage where there is domestic violence. It could be an ignorant manager or unfair working conditions (I've been there).

For others it could be an addiction to drugs or cigarettes. It could be growing up in the foster care system. It could be growing up in the streets of the projects. It could be living with parents who are alcoholics or drug users or physical abusers. It could be getting raped repeatedly by your mother or father or cousin or grandparent. It could be getting evicted from your home and being homeless. It could be losing a parent to the criminal justice system. It could be rejection by your father (my wife's cotton field) or your mother.

For someone else, it may be an incurable disease or cancer. For another, it may be the tribulation of trying to succeed in the middle of urban congestion, drugs, violence and crime. For others, it could be the problem of trying to deal with the loss of a loved one.

The question is *how* do you get back up when life seems to, not only knock you down but also kick you real hard *while* you are down. What do you do when *no one seems to have any answers? This is your cotton field!*

YOUR ENVIRONMENT OFTEN SHAPES YOU

Every person in this world was put here for a purpose. Clearly we are suppose to get a job, have a family, go to the movies, take vacations, have hobbies and go to church. We're also supposed to help others, properly raise our children, be good citizens, pay our bills and generally function in society, in a proper manner.

Yet, if we deeply look within and examine our likes, dislikes, strengths, weaknesses, habits and proclivities, we will begin to realize that there is some type of greater calling or mission God wants us to fulfill before we leave this earth. It may not be about acquiring millions of dollars. You may not be called to be the President of the United States, a world-class athlete, inventor, Pastor, writer or musician but there is something you are called to do to improve the world in which we live.

Sometimes it may not be easy to determine what your God given earthly assignment is. You may have to diligently seek and search to find out what that purpose is and live in a way that enables you to carry out that purpose. It's easier to look at world-renowned people to recognize what their calling may be. For example, who in the world would ever have the audacity to say Thomas Edison missed his calling? This man came up with more than one thousand inventions. What about George Washington Carver? He worked wonders with the peanut and other products.

"When it is dark enough, you can see the stars."
-Ralph Waldo Emerson

HOW WILL YOU RESPOND?

So what is *one* of your callings? **You are called to succeed**. No matter what your cotton field may be, you can be set free. Your cotton field may be physical, spiritual, financial, social or emotional. Whatever it may be, you do not have to live in your cotton field. **You can be set free**! The Bible says, whom the Son has set free is free indeed. That means me. That means you!

I would not be the man I am today without the cotton field. It built my character, my never give up attitude, my determination, my "fight for right" mindset, my persistence and my determination to succeed.

~~~~~~~~~~~~~~~~~~~~
What is your cotton field? How long are you going to stay in it?
You can't succeed in the future if you're trapped where you are.
~~~~~~~~~~~

CONQUER YOUR COTTON FIELD

"Hardships, trouble, tribulations and strife,

Are what we'll sometimes get in life.
Without the rain, the crops will cease,
Upset the world, disrupt the peace.
The Father with His guiding light,
Will see us through our darkest night.
Every burden, yoke, stumble or fall,
Can make the weak and low stand tall.
The battles that you fight and win
Will bring achievement in the end.
Hold on, be tough and don't give up,
SUCCESS will emerge from your bitter cup."

-Calvin Washington

We must all understand that there will be many challenges and struggles that we will face as we journey through life. The Word of God says, "In the world you will have trouble" (John 16:33 NIV).

That's just how life is. *Everyone has a proverbial cotton field.* Yours may be low self-esteem, heart trouble that runs in the family, trouble keeping a good job, trouble getting a college education and trouble finding a good spouse or trouble staying out of debt. Your cotton field may be wasteful spending, overeating, a very high temper, trouble with clutter, cigarette smoking, depression or never ending poverty regardless of what you do.

The good news is, *you can escape from your cotton field* just like I did. This is what John 16:33 says in its entirety, *"I have told you these things, so that in me you may have peace. In this world you will have trouble. But take heart! I have overcome the world."*

CONQUERING YOUR COTTON FIELD

PRAYER BY ITSELF

You can start your journey out of your cotton field and onto the road to success by using prayer by itself. If you labor before God in prayer and cry out to Him day, after day, He will eventually respond to your cry. The Bible says if you seek and search for God with all your heart, He will be found (Jeremiah 29:13). Just say, "Lord I seek You with all my heart to free me from_____.
(fill in the blank with whatever your situation may be). Say this over and over many times. Your prayer will be answered if you seek and don't quit!

PRAYER AND FASTING

Another great and powerful way to conquer your cotton field is to go before God with prayer combined with fasting. You can say this: "Lord it's my desire to overcome the struggle I have had trying to break the habit of _____. (fill in the blank with whatever your situation may be). I am going on a three day fast and I ask that You direct Your attention to my need through this fast. Use this fast to help me Lord, free me and deliver me from this habit. In the name of Jesus I pray."

You could use this same principle to get rid of trouble with a rebellious child, trouble with your next-door neighbors or trouble with managing money or basically any problem. I used prayer and fasting for my wedding to be great, joyous and successful. It may take a number of fasts but you will win if you continue the fight!

FIGHT THE GOOD FIGHT OF FAITH

Another way to fight your battle is through the use of your faith. Faith comes by speaking out loud what you desire. The Bible says, call those things that be not as though they were (Romans 4:17). **This means you have to say you already have what you want** *before* **you have it PHYSICALLY or EXPERIENTIALLY.**

For example, if your cotton field is trouble getting a good car say this, "Lord I receive Your gift of a good and reliable car in the name of Jesus." Then just say out loud many times, "Thank You God for blessing me with a good and reliable car." Keep saying this and you will get the required amount of faith to get the car.

When that faith shows up and comes into your heart, then the car will somehow show up, one way or the other. You can use this same principle to get rid of any mountain or cotton field in your life. I have done this and I have gotten great results many times. This is *how* you fight the good fight of faith!

~~~~~~~~~~~~~~~~~~~~~
Remember, no problem is too big for God.
~~~~~~~~~~~

You will eliminate the burden of your cotton field if you persist and keep moving forward. If God is for you, who can be against you? No one!

~~~~~~~~~~~~~~~~~~~~
With God all things are possible.
~~~~~~~~~~~

God is no respecter of persons. The scripture says, "Peter opened his mouth and said: Most certainly and thoroughly I now perceive and understand that God shows no partiality and is no respecter of persons" (Acts 10:34 AMP).

16

MY FINAL WORDS

**"If you know everything
there is to know in life, your name is God."
-Nicole Y. Washington**

It is NOT God's will for us to "JUST GET BY" in life. NO! That is absolutely WRONG! God wants us to REIGN as kings in life through Jesus Christ. We are to TAKE CHARGE in adverse and dire situations. God wants us to take the bull by the horns and drive the enemy away from us! **To make your way prosperous and have *good* success in life, implement these tips in your life:**

1. Know that it is God's will for you to succeed in life.
2. Recognize that God is your true source of success.
3. Seek God first instead of things, success will follow.
4. Obey God's Word. Do what Jesus said.
5. Don't think wrong, talk wrong or act wrong.
6. Be a giver and not a taker. If you have been obedient to give, then expect to receive.
7. Have a good attitude filled with godly expectations of success.
8. Use wisdom in every area of your life. Wisdom brings success.
9. You can serve God and have money, *if* you will use money the way God intended. It's great to have things as long as things don't have you.

10. Fear will produce the very thing you fear, the same way faith will produce the very thing you believe.

11. When you pray, focus on the desired outcome instead of the problem.

12. Believe, don't doubt and you will succeed.

13. God wants to use His power and ability on your behalf. He wants you to walk in success—spiritually, physically, financially, socially and emotionally.

14. Success requires diligence, dedication and determination.

15. Don't get trapped by the words of your own mouth.

16. Make giving a habit because you've got to sow before you can reap.

17. If you see trouble coming your way, speak to it and command it to go, in the name of Jesus.

18. Always forgive. Unforgiveness and strife are spiritual problems that can cause physical illness.

19. You can't tame your tongue but you sure can control it with the help of God. Exercise control of your vocabulary. Be mindful of what you say.

20. You reap what you sow whether good or bad.

21. Conquer your "cotton field." Do whatever you can to break free. Your destiny awaits.

22. Whatever you say, over and over, is what you will get.

23. Dare to daydream with God. Reach for the stars and you just might get stardust.

24. Be content but not complacent.

25. Destroy the success blockers in your life.

26. Things that are seen today are subject to change tomorrow. Remember, with faith all things are possible.

27. An opportunity is a bridge that rewards you when it's crossed.
28. Change your thoughts, change your attitude, change your day, it will change your life.
29. A great attitude is like a crane that lifts you toward the sky.
30. God has called you to succeed so never, never, ever, give up on that call!

Most people will never *experience* success. They'll *think* about it, *dream* about it and *talk* about it but they won't *live* it! Why?

They don't realize they are *called to succeed* and don't know *how* to walk in that calling. *You* were once like *them* but *not* anymore. After reading this book and putting into action the truths that lie herein, it is now time for you to *step out* and *step up*, reach higher and further than *ever* before, to fulfill what has been eluding you for years, *Success!*

THE RACE AT SUNRISE

Every morning in Africa, a gazelle wakes up.

It knows that it must run faster than the fastest lion or it will be killed.

Every morning a lion wakes up. It knows that it must outrun the slowest gazelle or it will starve to death.

It doesn't matter whether you are a lion or a gazelle,

When the sun comes up, you had better be running.

-African Parable

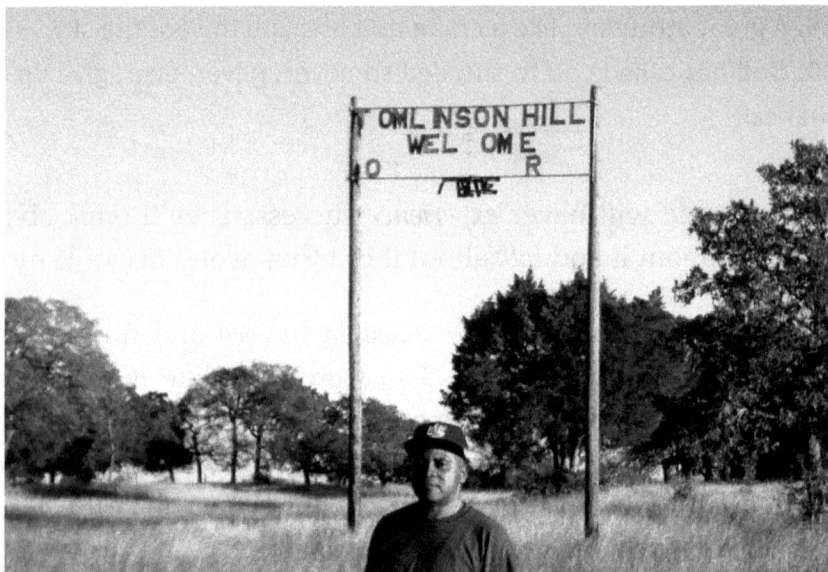

Calvin Washington in front of the
Tomlinson Hill Welcome Sign,
Falls County Texas

17

CALVIN WASHINGTON

By Nicole Y. Washington

"I have learned that success is to be measured not so much by the position that one has reached in life as by the obstacles which one has overcome while trying to succeed."
-Booker T. Washington

In a *very small* central Texas community called Tomlinson Hill, Calvin Washington was born to Mr. & Mrs. Patrick and Inez Washington, the seventh of eight children. Growing up in rural central Texas, near Waco, Calvin was born into a life of poverty that most of us would find *absolutely incredible*.

His parents were cotton pickers and laborers. Agrarian work was commonplace in his community. At age 6, Calvin was picking cotton along with the rest of the family in the hot, blazing, unforgiving Texas sun. This was the means of his family's survival. By the time he was a teenager, besides picking cotton, he was also hauling hay, picking watermelons, "chopping cotton" (clearing the weeds from the cotton plant), picking tomatoes and harvesting pecans.

Now, in your minds, you may envision him gathering a few

watermelons, several tomatoes, a few sacks of cotton, etc. If so, your picture would be *extremely* out of focus. When he picked watermelons, it was not 50 or 60; it was more like 500 to 600 per day. When he picked cotton, it was not like 5 or 6 pounds (remember one cotton boll is almost weightless), it was more like 500 to 600 pounds of cotton a day. The workday involved almost nonstop, intensive physical work, for 12 or 13 hours a day. These work hours were called "sun up to sun down."

Calvin would have *treasured* many of the things we took for granted when we were growing up. Although his parents purchased land, his home was on a dirt (sandy) road. There was *no indoor plumbing* at his home. To get water for drinking, bathing and washing clothes, the family had to pull water up from a well about 50 yards away, by using a tin bucket.

Without indoor running water, the family was relegated to using a privy (*outhouse*) in lieu of an indoor toilet. His family never used the phone because there was none in their home to use. They never slammed doors inside because there were none to slam. His mother divided rooms with sheets. They used a large galvanized tub to bathe in. They did have a car but it generally would not start without being pushed by hand or pulled by another vehicle to get the engine to start.

"The greatest motivation in life is when someone puts the impossible before you and you challenge the impossible against all odds."
-Unknown

It was not until the *late 60's* that his home had an indoor toilet, hot water and even a bathtub for the first time. Extreme poverty and cultural barriers were just a part of daily life on the "Hill" (Tomlinson Hill).

Although Calvin grew up in extreme poverty, his parents did an excellent job of raising him and his siblings. Mr. and Mrs. Washington taught their children to live honest, moral, righteous lives. Each child was taught to work hard and have a very strong work ethic. His parents were economically and financially limited by poor educational backgrounds and the oppressive conditions in the era in which they lived. In spite of these conditions, his parents did a great job, as they were outstanding, exemplary and loving parents.

During many hours of isolation, bending and toiling in the cotton field, Calvin, who *hated each moment spent* in the cotton field, began to dream of his exodus. The burning questions in his soul were: How do I escape this? How do I escape the injustice my family endures? How do I escape poverty and lack? How do I escape deprivation and inequality?

Calvin continued to dream of escape from those cotton fields. As the years passed, nothing to the visible eye was changing but he continued to dream. He would dream of freedom and success. He wanted to be free of cotton, free of poverty, free of racism, free of social injustice and free of oppression.

For kids growing up on the Hill, dropping out of school was all too common. Calvin found a book at school one day on Black History. That was the turning point in his life. As he worked in the cotton field, hauled hay and gutted turkeys, he kept reading that book over and over. He learned from Harriet Tubman and Fredrick Douglass as well as others, to never give up on his dreams. All he wanted was a life that had, to that point, eluded him, one including the basic dignities of American life.

He knew there had to be something better to life than the existence he had. College was the only means of escape he could imagine, so he set his heart and mind on being the first college graduate of his family. His dedication and determination to achieve that goal was unshakable, (although he was physically still in the cotton fields) and eventually became undeniable. Being valedictorian of his high school class, he won a state tuition scholarship to Prairie View A&M University.

"The greater the obstacle, the more glory in overcoming it."
-Molière

Overcoming the enormous challenges of attending college from a substandard educational system, based on prejudice and racism, Calvin successfully graduated from Prairie View A&M University with an ROTC background and went to the Army as a second lieutenant. During this time, the dream he had while in the cotton field continued. He was not content.

There was still more for him. He was not *far enough away* from the cotton field yet.

Because of an encounter a family member had with the legal system that was unfair and unjust, Calvin decided to become a lawyer. Although there was no money in sight, he was not deterred. He won a Martin Luther King Jr. fellowship to attend Howard University Law School. As a result of his stellar academic achievement, he was given the honor of writing for the Howard Law Journal.

After successfully graduating from law school and becoming a member of the State Bar of Texas, he was at that point, a little bit further from the cotton field. The sweet savor of success, the ability to create a new life, was on the horizon.

He received a rude awakening as he found that jobs were very scarce. Searching for a job became a job itself. He had to get a job at a fast food chicken restaurant to get money for gas to adequately search for a legal job. That job became another cotton field in his life.

Working beneath his capabilities, he was laughed at by coworkers and misused by his managers. Again, the passion of hatred for the literal cotton field he had just escaped, began to rage against the figurative cotton field he was in at the restaurant. Escape was soon at hand.

Eventually, he did get a job with the U.S. Government as a staff attorney. Later, he got a job working for another agency. Yet again, given the hard work, stress and challenges, he found himself in another figurative cotton field. Not to be defeated in life, he used the same escape methods he used back on the Hill and at the chicken restaurant, to escape yet again. Escape, he did!

~~~~~~~~~~~~~~~~~~~~
Calvin is currently an Administrative Law Judge with the Federal Government and now a great distance from the cotton fields of rural Falls County Texas!
~~~~~~~~~~~

Calvin and I began our ministry together in San Antonio TX, by founding Triumphant Ministries International. Not long after that, we formed a publishing company and wrote our bestseller, "Confessing the Word of God."

Later, in metro Atlanta GA, Calvin began his first position as a Federal Administrative Judge. While there, he founded his first church, Shiloh Christian Fellowship in Riverdale GA and was there until a job promotion took him to Montgomery AL.

While in Montgomery, we founded Revelation Church where we pastored. During those years many people were ordained; churches and ministries were planted. Revelation Church currently operates in the metro Atlanta area.

Calvin is also the founder, with me, of Success Factory Ministries. The Success Factory, a network of Pastors and Ministers and an outreach of Revelation Church, is a cutting-edge, left of tradition, Spirit-led, no holds barred, "for today" ministry, cut and sewn by God, perfectly tailored to those who need to know "how to" live successfully.

Our belief is that success should be seen in your education, your career, your home and your marriage, parenting your kids and sometimes parenting your parents!

~~~~~~~~~~~~~~~~~~~~
Calvin's mission and mandate is simple and clear - THE ADVANCEMENT OF THE KINGDOM through the attainment of natural, spiritual and all around success!
~~~~~~~~~~~

He shares the tools, knowledge and rules of the game that are required to achieve personal and public success.

The mantra of his life is:
For every problem God's got a solution.
So never, never, ever give up on God,
yourself or your dream!

YOU TOO,
ARE CALLED TO SUCCEED!

"Only believe! God will not fail you, Beloved. It is impossible for God to fail. Believe Him. Rest in Him, for God's rest is an undisturbed place where heaven bends to meet you. God will fulfill the promises made to you in His Word—believe it!"
-Smith Wigglesworth

"In the end,
"It's not the years in your life that count.
It's the life in your years."
-Abraham Lincoln

"By perseverance the snail reached the ark."
-Charles Spurgeon

"An unused life is an early death."
-Chinese Proverb

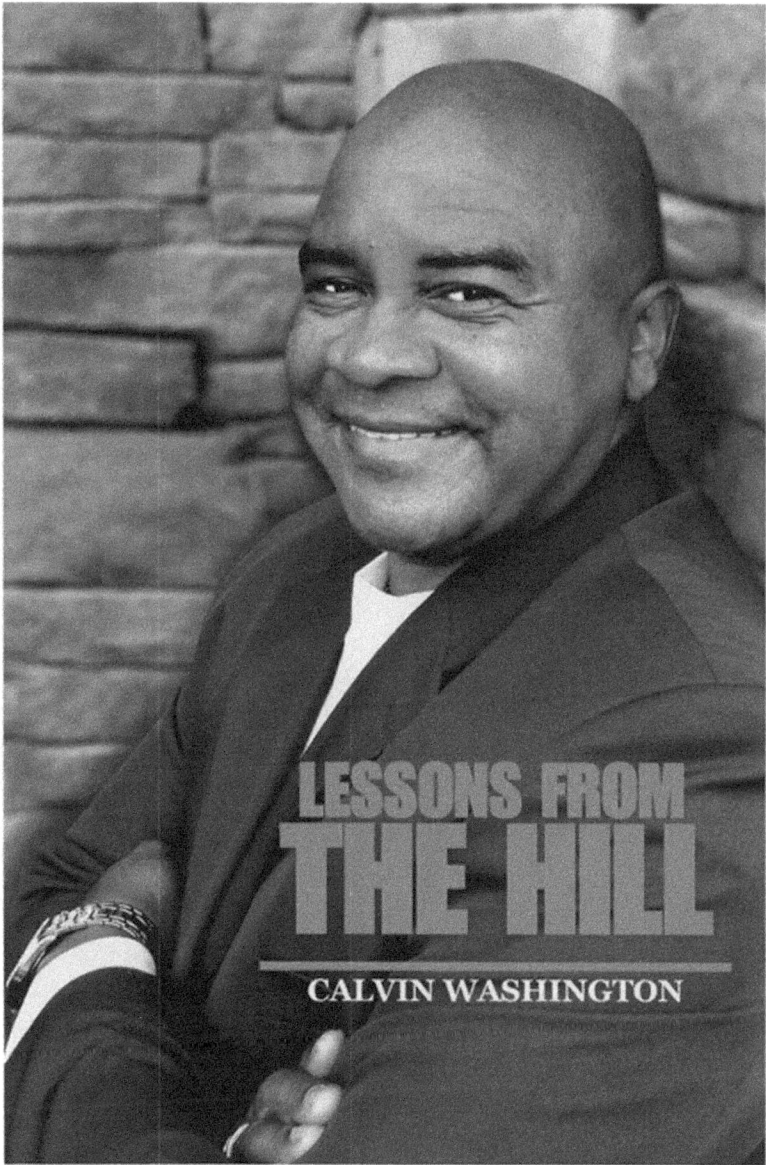

LESSONS FROM THE HILL

THE HILL

CALVIN WASHINGTON

LESSONS FROM THE HILL:
100 INSIGHTS THAT WILL CHANGE
THE WAY YOU LIVE YOUR LIFE

COMING SUMMER 2014

LLAMADO PARA TENER ÉXITO

CALVIN WASHINGTON

CALLED TO SUCCEED IS AVAILABLE IN SPANISH AS
LLAMADO PARA TENER ÉXITO AND ALSO AVAILABLE IN
LARGE PRINT AND AS AN EBOOK
FROM AMAZON.COM

To Contact Calvin Washington

For Speaking Engagements, Conferences, Business
Meetings, Interviews and all other media inquiries:
Devon Chenee Media, LLC
Email: devon@devonchenee.com

MAIL:
11877 Douglas Road, Suite 102213
Johns Creek, GA 30005

E-MAIL: info@calvinwashington.com
WEB: www.judgewashington.com

PHONE: 678.490.1016

Disclaimer:

Calvin Washington and the staffs of Revelation Church, The Success Factory and Washington Publications are prohibited from addressing a person's legal matters by phone, fax, e-mail, Facebook, twitter or any other means of communication.

Please refer questions related to your legal matters to your own attorney or legal group.

www.ingramcontent.com/pod-product-compliance
Lightning Source LLC
Chambersburg PA
CBHW071527040426
42452CB00008B/908